STRIKE YOUR CROWD!

HOW TO MANAGING CROWDFUNDING IN FUNDRAISING CAMPAIGNS FOR BUSINESS AND INVESTMENTS

© Copyright 2020 by ProBusiness Publishing

All rights reserved.

This document is geared towards providing exact and reliable information with regards to the topic and issue covered. The publication is sold with the idea that the publisher is not required to render accounting, officially permitted, or otherwise, qualified services. If advice is necessary, legal or professional, a practiced individual in the profession should be ordered.

- From a Declaration of Principles which was accepted and approved equally by a Committee of the American Bar Association and a Committee of Publishers and Associations.

In no way is it legal to reproduce, duplicate, or transmit any part of this document in either electronic means or in printed format. Recording of this publication is strictly prohibited and any storage of this document is not allowed unless with written permission from the publisher. All rights reserved.

The information provided herein is stated to be truthful and consistent, in that any liability, in terms of inattention or otherwise, by any usage or abuse of any policies, processes, or directions contained within is the solitary and utter responsibility of the recipient reader. Under no circumstances will any legal responsibility or blame be held against the publisher for any reparation, damages, or monetary loss due to the information herein, either directly or indirectly.

Respective authors own all copyrights not held by the publisher.

The information herein is offered for informational purposes solely, and is universal as so. The presentation of the information is without contract or any type of guarantee assurance.
The trademarks that are used are without any consent, and the publication of the trademark is without permission or backing by the trademark owner. All trademarks and brands within this book are for clarifying purposes only and are the owned by the owners themselves, not affiliated with this document

Page left intentionally blank

Table of Contents

- INTRODUCTION 7
- HOW CROWDFUNDING WORKS 8
    - Understanding Crowdsourcing 8
    - The Power of the Crowd - Thoughts to Make You Think 16
    - Crowdfunding & Its Benefits, Effects 19
    - The Pros and Cons of Crowdfunding 21
    - Is Crowdfunding Right for Your Business Idea? 24
- TYPES OF CROWDFUNDING 26
    - Types Of Crowdfunding 26
    - Crowdfunding: How Your Nonprofit Can Get Started 30
    - How To Craft a Successful Crowdfunding Pitch 32
- PLATFORMS FOR CROWDFUNDING 34
    - Platforms For Crowdfunding 34
    - Fundamentals of Crowdfunding 38
    - Crowdfunding Your Way to Financing 39
    - Anatomy of a Startup: Raising Money 41
- CROWDFUNDING CAMPAIGN 46
    - Crowdfunding Campaign 46
    - You Created a Crowdfunding Campaign, Now What? 47
    - Important Things You Must Know Before Commencing A Crowdfunding Campaign 51
    - Crowdfunding Tips For Non-Profits 53
    - Raising Capital With Crowdfunding 55
- CREATING AN AUDIENCE (CROWDFUNDING AUDIENCE) 57
    - The Perfect Audience 57

- How to Grab Your Audiences' Attention Instantly 59
- 5 Dynamic Thoughts to Engage Your Audience 62

GOAL SETTINGS (CROWDFUNDING GOAL) 66
- Five Tips for Successful Crowdfunding 66
- The Importance of Goal Setting 72
- Helping a Cause Through Crowdfunding 75
- How To Do Business Through Crowdfunding 78
- Crowdfunding Using Fundly 79

TIMING (CROWDFUNDING TIMING) 82
- Time to Consider Crowdsourcing 82
- At Ease on Stage - How to Connect With the Crowd 84
- How to Choose Your Event Timing System 85
- The Concept Of Crowd Funding 89
- Crowdfunding - The Social Way To Raise Funds 91

AFTER THE LAUNCH (CROWDFUNDING LAUNCH) 94
- Beyond Raising Capital 94
- Common Crowdfunding Problems and Solutions After The Launch 95
- How to Prepare for a Crowdfunding Project After The Launch 97
- Using Social Media for Raising Funds 98

CAMPAIGN CONCLUSION (CROWDFUNDING CAMPAIGN) 102
- Effective Ways of Non-Profit Fund Raising Year Around 102
- Crowdfunding for a Business Is More Than Just Money 107
- Finance Your Startup in the Community 112
- Equity Crowdfunding: Set to Change the World 119

DELIVER THE REWARDS – (CROWDFUNDING FULFILLMENT) 122
- What's the Next Step If Your Crowdfunding Campaign Fails? 12222

Three Powerful Tricks To Slingshot Your Crowdfunding Campaign . 125

Is Crowdfunding Right For Your Non-Profit?................................... 12626

Things to Consider When Crowdfunding for Charity 128

CONCLUSION.. 131

INTRODUCTION

Imagine a crowd that could all have a positive ability to change the world. Think if it could possibly be possible for a group of people to heal the planet by all thinking that the planet is already healed. Think of five people, all focusing simultaneously on a good positive outcome. Imagine the good which might come into the world if people could positively change the world just by all thinking of the good thing.

We also go to other locations, such as malls, airports, and banks. And you always find everything to organize; people waiting for their turn in their respective queues. Crowd Control is the reason for this control of patience.

Crowd Control is achieved by-products from Crowd Control that support the organization and management of the crowd. What are Crowd Control Devices exactly? They are simple, elegant, and effective ways to ensure that the decorum is preserved with heavyweights. Crowd Control devices are various types, and the most common are Crowd Control or Stanchion posts, these compact and sturdy posts hold the people in a queue from switching sides, they are also used to deter people from entering locations outside the borders of the general public when you set up a new queue or test the existing queue structure's effectiveness.

Most people are going to ask, "Why do we have to control the crowd?" Imagine sitting at a ticket office or an information booth where Crowd Control's products are not available. You would be in a position to react to several people in the same case. This will not help everybody and everybody to get what they need.

Understanding Crowdsourcing

Have any of you ever heard the word multi-faceted? You are probably familiar with the crowdsourcing process, even if you can't remember hearing that word before. Crowdsourcing is the collection of public information, and it is then used to complete a related business task. This information is then used through partnership or opposition by a broad community of people. Crowdsourcing offers the company the ability to easily and efficiently pursue new ideas. They are able to leverage resources beyond the organization, and this will help to generate additional potential benefits.

Crowdsourcing is particularly popular as well as convenient for Internet use. For businesses and for customers, as they can quickly submit their feedback and share their opinions on the product of the business. Crowdfunding is a form of crowdfunding. "The electronic call for money from a dispersed audience, and in exchange, offers a new means for people or teams to ask for help from a dispersed audience." The article shows that conventional ways of fundraising, such as seeking funds from institutions, change through sites such as "Go Fund Me."

Crowd votes are another form of crowdsourcing. "Crowd voting is a crowdsourcing process in which a platform promotes or sells only those goods and services which have the support of the majority of the digital crowd." Crowd-voting is a means of expressing opinion only from the community, which is interested in a given issue.

The third and final instance of crowdsourcing I'm talking about is a crowd competition. "The easiest way to get a crowd involved is to create a contest. The sponsor or company identifies a particular problem, offers a cash prize, and calls for solutions. Contests work well because it isn't clear what mix of expertise or even what technical strategy can contribute to the best solution to a problem. "The conducting of competition is close to the checking of the outcomes, but we see several variations in performance.

Hopefully, we can now understand more easily the term "crowdsourcing" and realize the difference between at least three different types of crowdsourcing. On a personal note from all the crowdsourcing types, I feel that crowd competitions are among the most effective crowdsourcing methods.

How crowdfunding works

Crowdfunding will be all the rage with ever more new platforms. Many viewings are related as an investment future; others warn which risks are frequently underestimated. And then you have various crowdfunding types: premium, equity, flexible, debt-based, fixed, etc. It may all sound complicated, but the underlying logic is plain, like most things.

The main advantage of crowdfunding would be that it makes investments in small firms and startups accessible to all. This is why it is important more than ever for people to understand this new world since the main focus of the negative publicity all over crowdfunding is the misuse and misunderstanding of the platforms. In this chapter, I will cover the various types of crowdfunding platforms and the main incumbents of each category and explain some of the main falls on many newcomers.

First, however, there is a definition.

What is the crowd?

Every day, ordinary people. And this is what the crowd refers to in crowdfunding. You see, raising money really isn't about corporate plans or market traction or financial projections: it is about trust, ultimately. And in life, the greater the risk of injury, the greater the trust. This is why most people do not care to sponsor a charity run or lend a friend a couple of pounds; they accept that you should not expect to see that money again, so the confidence in the person you are paying is not particularly high. However, if someone asks you to invest thousands of pounds, the situation is radically different. It is not an amount of money for most people that they should afford to lose. Most people were, therefore, locked out of the world of investment, where small businesses require thousands of pounds to invest.

Thus, it is logical for founders to finance a business to have traditional routes like banks' loans, high net worth persons, and friends and family. The ability of a founder to raise money largely depended on his collateral for the bank lending, or his personal network for individual investments, and consisted of large pieces of money from small groups of individuals who trusted in it or thoroughly examined it. The alternative-raising small pieces of money from many people-is largely impossible unless the founder knows hundreds of people and can deal with the huge administrative burden of dealing with so many people.

Enter the Internet with a long history of removing administrative headaches and connecting large numbers of people with each other. Crowdfunding mainly facilitates interaction between ordinary people interested in investing in things and ordinary founders who do not have access to collateral or large networks of wealthy people. The software running the crowdfunding platform controls the entire administration, and the Internet itself provides the founder with a vast potential bundle of people to market on a scale.

In short, crowdfunding enables a large number of total strangers to raise small amounts of money. It's great for that reason.

The main crowdfunding platform types

There are four main crowdfunding platforms, all with various advantages and risks. Below are the only ones with ties to the largest or the most popular incumbents.

Crowdfunding based on rewards

Main players: Indiegogo, Kickstarter

The closest brother to the conventional charitable donors, reward-based sites, are collecting money in the form of commitments or gifts, and in exchange, you get some kind of turnaround from the business. For instance, you can get a discounted unit of the product funded after it is made, or a customized version of the same product as a thank you for supporting it for a higher donation sum. That is the "reward" and the bigger the gift, the greater the reward.

For obvious purposes, you continue to see more tangible items at incentives, where the money is used to create a project prototype. They are also popular in creative projects like films, games, and music albums where fans can help their favorite artists and receive rewards such as a credit at the end of the film.

The downside is that they have been vulnerable to scams and theft. It is usually little, or no due diligence in collecting money from companies or individuals, and the minimum promise amount starting at £ 1 is also minimal. Scammers often present fake product prototypes in a video showing concept art and returns, only to vanish with money when the campaign is over. In this case, investors have few recourses except to complain about the crowdfunding platform itself, but risk lines are somewhat hazy.

There are fantastic possibilities to support exciting projects on rewarding platforms, but the risk is greatest, and the return is generally not appreciable. Investment on a reward-oriented platform should be made out of a passion for the product you are investing in rather than expected financial returns.

Crowdfunding based on equity

Main players: Crowdcube, Seedrs

Although closer to the conventional idea of finance, stock-based systems promote investing in businesses in return for shares in these firms. The Financial Ethics Regulator in the United Kingdom controls stock platforms, and creditors have to comply with those regulatory requirements. However, they are not particularly rigorous and usually involve simply checking credit and completing an online survey. Minimum investment sums at about £10 typically remain very open, although some equity markets have higher minimum stakes.

However, the entry process is much tougher for companies that want to raise. Every company has the right legal, due diligence, and the submission procedure usually consists of a number of iterations and approval rounds before the campaign can go live. The added security shield of their wealth is a clear benefit for investors. It is much rarer for fraudsters or assailants to launch equity platforms, and FCA regulations require companies to support claims with proof that the platform will verify itself before the campaign is started. This is why up to 90 percent of all equity-based platform applications do not succeed in launching the campaign.

The advantages of money-raising businesses are the access to a more advanced group of investors outside of their own networks (traditional investors flock to such platforms increasingly) and a simplified process for dealing with the group of investors, which generally is much smaller than other crowd financing platforms. There is also an increasing trend towards stock platforms operating as designated shareholders on behalf of founders, making the company much easier to run, as well as to make prospective acquisitions much easier to take on a single new shareholder rather than several hundred. Often businesses want to raise this particular issue overlooked, but this is the main reason that we chose Seedrs for our own fundraising campaign.

Equity platforms will usually keep the funds in check until the campaign ends and add an additional layer of investor protection. Naturally, the normal risks relate to expected returns: most investments will return little if nothing, but those that promise huge financial gains in comparison to other investment options. In general, the speculation about the impact of the format on the future of investing generally refers to this type of crowdfunding.

Crowdfunding based on debt

Key players: Circle of Support, Zopa

Debt-based crowdfunding otherwise referred to as peer-to-peer loans, take the key advantages of crowdfunding-the administrative benefits and access for large groups of people-and applies to business lends. Simply put, investors place their money into a platform-managed fund, and the platform lends the money to companies seeking capital. Investors could either choose whether companies they want to invest in or have the platform selected on their behalf automatically.

Of course, the main difference is that the investor should expect the money back with interest. The call for money to be placed on a bank-based lending platform instead of a shareholder comes down to the reduced risk factor, which guarantees that companies are treated as rigorously as bank loans and that returns are often far higher than ISA or pension schemes. For a company that fulfills the loan criteria, the advantages are better than a bank with greater transparency.

While commonly not ideal besides early-stage startups without guarantees, it provides cash for more established companies who want to grow without hundreds of investors having to give up equity. This represents a safer alternative to equity crowdfunding for more risk-averse investment at the cost of missing potentially large returns that successful startups may sometimes yield.

Crowdfunding Blockchain

Highlights: Smith + Cap, Waves

Blockchain crowdfunding is the newest and lesser established kind of crowdfunding, which utilizes the power of cryptocurrencies like Bitcoin to raise cash through the creation of new tokens called Initial Coin Offers (ICOs), the node to our more conventional Initial Public Offering (IPO) method.

It is quite difficult to explain the way it works, and it is essential to understand how Blockchain and cryptocurrencies function before contemplating this path. As such, the companies raising money through this route are largely blockchain-related, and investors in the ICOs tend to be very risky.

The value lies in the future gains for investors themselves from crystal currencies. For example, during March 2017, the Ether cryptocurrency doubled in price in only three days, with the Monero currency increasing in value by 2000 percent last year alone. Naturally, this level of volatility could also go the other way as anyone who has recently invested in Bitcoin will prove.

The decentralized architecture of Blockchain and its trustless, cross-funded approach is a clear candidate in the future for preferred crowdfunding, but the technology as a whole is still early on and as such prone to scammers and fraud, as well as huge turnover. Not for faint-hearted men.

Which one are you supposed to choose?

As an investor, the opportunity to buy in the crowdfunding platform largely depends on your appetite for risk. If you wish to earn some payout, the compensation systems should be absolutely omitted. Furthermore, if you are only searching for a better interest rate to sell than ISA, debt-based projects that be a reasonable choice, then you would prefer to be a real investment if you are searching for a capital crowdfunding alternative. Blockchain is for gamblers. For gamblers.

As a company, stick to reward-based consumer platforms that are on the stage of conception or prototype, perhaps move onto equity platforms once the product is ready. When you are more mature, debt-based mechanisms are a safer option for bridge funding, and Blockchain is the obvious solution, but if you're a Blockchain startup.

Whatever the stage you are, make sure you shop around and research before you dive in, and there are great opportunities as long as it keeps a sensible head. That is why crowdfunding itself is a wonderful invention.

The Power of the Crowd - Thoughts to Make You Think

Imagine that a crowd could all have a positive potential to change the world. Think about how it would be possible for a community of people to cure the world simply by assuming that the earth has already been healed. Think of five people, all focusing simultaneously on a good positive outcome. Imagine the positive that could come into the world if people will actually change the environment only by dreaming about a single optimistic idea, all at once.

Imagine that an audience has the ability to bring love into the world by concentrating all at once on positive results. Imagine if words can come to life, think if you can create what you think of every time you think. This means you just have to worry about positive outcomes because anything you worried about will happen.

Perhaps it is good that the things we think about don't happen when we think about them.

If we could make something happen as we think about them, we'd have to be accountable. We'd have to be vigilant of the things we were talking of. We should be careful not to say inappropriate or disagreeable ideas.

And, if what we dreamed about occurred the moment we dreamed of it, would that be a positive thing? Or if we had not the power to regulate our thoughts, this might be a concern.

Imagine that we existed again after we die, in a world where we manifested everything we needed merely by dreaming about it.

What would you like to create, and what would you like to see?

Can a mass of people bring about change by reflecting on this result simultaneously? Napoleon Hill spoke about the Master Mind philosophy, the notion of people who meet in peace daily and find solutions to problems. He spoke about the fact that when people work together in peace, they can do a lot. As the saying suggests, they tend to achieve a lot more when people are united.

Controlling the Masses Without Monarchy

Crowd Control is achieved by-products from Crowd Control that help to organize and manage crowds. What is Crowd Control Products exactly? They are simple, elegant, and effective ways of ensuring that the decorum is kept in large areas. There are several various forms of Crowd Management products; Crowd Control Post or Stanchion posts are the most common, these compact and durable posts keep people in a queue from defecting and are often used to restrict access to areas outside the boundaries of the crowd. When you set up a new queue or check your current queue structure effectiveness. We would say that there are four main factors:

1. Your customer flow predictability

Will the business have a high consumer volume? The flow and volume of customers determine the correct structure and influence many factors, from the required floor space to the formation of the queue.

2. The goods or services you have

First, what's that? Products or products? The answer to this question alone has an effect on the structure and strategies that you use in the queue. The characteristics will help you determine whether a traditional queue or an electronic call-forward queue, whether you concentrate on the tailor virtual queuing and whether you require multiple lines or a single line queue.

3. The clients you serve

Who in the line is waiting? In general, people are willing to wait longer for products or services of higher value, but less costly or commodified items may not be considered worth a long wait.

4. The experience you are trying to bring

What do you want to remind your customers about your business and queue? No matter what group you want your company to fall in, the queue needs focus. If you want to offer your customers speed, the flow and efficiency of the queue will probably be your primary focus.

The queue involves the knowledge of customers, their customers, and their demographics.

Now let's get to learn more about the barriers/posts on Crowd Management. What is a stanchion post exactly? A stagnant post is a robust upright post, often not a permanent fixture, and can be removed whenever necessary. The Crowd control panels are available in various types, including removable loops, double loops, classic clothes, chain, stand-alone units, floor sockets, and floor mounts, etc. They are made of bronze, silver, stainless steel, powder.

Crowdfunding & Its Benefits, Effects

What does crowdfunding mean?

As a contractor, your financial search can take various forms before the app ever reaches the market. If you've succeeded in the Friends and Family Round, you've probably made enough money to start developing your app.

So, what are you doing once you have used up the relatively small capital that the Friends and Family Round generates?

The next logical step in your search for funding is crowdfunding. Crowdfunding is a powerful tool that has been born on the web and powered by 'the crowd' since its inception. The process generates capital from investments made by crowdfunders like Kickstarter and Indiegogo.

The process of fundraising does not differ significantly between the competitions. However, there are variations in the way related charges are treated, and in the conditions that must be fulfilled in order to efficiently collect the capital produced.

What are the advantages?

It is a user base that makes crowdfunding such a strong platform for fundraising while the crowdfunding community is far more likely to fail to understand your vision, your family, and some of your friends.

Some backers are supporting people they have admired for a long time. Many people are just inspired by a new idea. Some are inspired by a project award — a copy of what is made, a small edition, or a customized experience related to the project. "– Kickstarter.

The popularity of this process means that many potential investors are patrolling the different crowdfunding platforms. That means that your project will probably be noticed by members of the "crowd." The vast user bases of these sites also mean that the amount of money you can produce can be quite large or very small, depending on your needs.

What are the dangers?

One of the least dangerous fundraising strategies is the crowdfunding round. There will be no drawbacks, depending on the choice of site. When you achieve your goal, most crowdfunding platforms take a percentage of your income. It would be useful to remember this when determining the minimum investment requirement of your campaign.

Some campaigns provide you with a choice of how the funding process is conducted. For example, Indiegogo gives you two options: adjustable finance and fixed financing. Both solutions take 4% of your income if you hit your target. However, if you choose flexible funding, Indiegogo maintains 9% of your earnings if you do not reach your goal. However, if you don't reach your goal, you can have zero for set financing, and Indiegogo returns all of your earnings to creditors.

This should be borne in mind as you prepare your fundraising strategy-if you don't meet your goal, you will end up with inadequate funding and 9 percent more.

The Pros and Cons of Crowdfunding

Today, a growing number of startups, but instead, artists are using the so-called crowdfunding phenomenon. Crowdfunding describes the co-operative initiative of individuals who network and share their resources on the Internet in order to support persons or organizations' efforts. Crowdfunding has been used to finance a variety of initiatives, including disaster relief, fans' musician's sponsorship, election campaigns, startup businesses, films, and the production of free software.

Of course, the enormous potential of crowdfunding can be seen. Crowdfunding means allowing more people to realize their dreams and ideas since its beginning in 2009. Kickstarter was able to raise $203 million in the last six months alone, and it does not appear to slow down.

Many crowdfunding platforms like Indiegogo, Crowdfunder, RocketHub, and Crowdrise are all heading towards the same growth and popularity.

While crowdfunding may seem to be a fantasy for any startup, a smart entrepreneur must still consider the pros and cons before opting to use this approach to collect money.

The Income

Enterprises from around the world can bear witness to the struggles and difficulties of accessing capital to finance new companies. Crowd-based funding is a perfect option to venture capital as people can do so without giving up or raising debt. Instead, companies may donate goods or gifts to the funding group, also known as reward-based crowdfunding, in place of money.

Moreover, crowdfunding platforms are an excellent way to market and raise awareness of a new business. Typically, these sites are free and offer a wide range of options for reaching a large number of people. For example, companies can promote themselves and their missions via social media channels, word of mouth, and increased transfer to their company website.

One of the main advantages of crowd financing is that it enables companies to receive consumer feedback earlier. Effective businesses use consumer ideas to develop their procedures, products, or services. Sadly, these changes are sometimes made way too late in the game, causing the business to fail. This anguish can be eliminated by crowdfunding by enabling entrepreneurs to assess customer reactions, promote user ideas, and test the product before it even hits the market. This not only saves a company from a large financial loss, but it also shows that a company is prepared and willing to listen to its customers straight from the bat.

The Context

Even though crowdfunding has many benefits, there are also some drawbacks. This method of funding, for example, exposes a contractor's idea and detailed insider information to potential competitors. This increases the risk of copying or stolen the idea of the owner, in particular, if the competition does have better financing.

Another disadvantage of crowdfunding is that it is not a viable way of financing long term. Although it is great to finance small, one-off projects, it is not great to generate on-going cash flow. However, businesses should also use crowdfunding as an extra method for fundraising, a particular project necessity, for example, a promotional event.

In addition, the amount of money a company can raise is limited. Crowdfunding covers the highest amount that can be collected in every 12-month period at $1 million. This is an enormous downside as most startups need more than that to get off the ground. This would benefit most companies far more if they were to seek a substantial amount of capital from angel investors or venture capitalists.

Although crowdfunding offers many benefits, such as increased access to capital, better brand visibility, and direct consumer feedback, one must be cautious. Entrepreneurs need to weigh up the positives and pitfalls of this approach before taking any practical fundraising decisions. Keep in mind that crowdfunding opens the project to competition, restricts the sum to be collected, and is inefficient in raising permanent money. When you have weighed these considerations, make sure you make the correct decision for your company

Is Crowdfunding Right for Your Business Idea?

There are many ways to try to get business funding. You can use credit cards, receive a conventional loan, raise equity from your house, or use crowdfunding. Crowdfunding offers many companies a great opportunity, but how do you know it's the right idea for your company?

Have you got a good plan? -- To set up a crowdfunding campaign, you need a very solid business plan, regardless of which type of funding you want. The reason is that it is important for investors to provide information about the work you have done, done, and done for your business. Don't try to get crowdfunding if you don't have a real business plan.

Do you know the amount of money you need? -- You will understand exactly how much money you have to raise when you have created a better business plan. You can't do the crowdfunding campaign if you don't realize how much you need, because you have to ask how much you want it to function.

Can you make donors or creditors a good bid? -- When you finance equity, how much equity will you give up for your total needs? It is not likely that many people will be interested if you do not give up a good percentage of your equity in exchange for the amount you need. If you are financing the type of reward, you can try to offer your donors something worthwhile.

How do you feel about crowdfunding in your target market? -- In some cases, you can hate the idea and lose faith in your target market. This isn't because crowdfunding is bad, but because some people don't. You can consider an education campaign before you do it, if so.

Are you ready for a marketing plan? -- It won't raise money by itself once you set up your crowdfunding campaign. You are the sole marketer of your campaign. You should also consider this in your budget because paid advertising is the best way to get the word out.

Can you invest too much? -- You would not have money, but you should be prepared to do the work required to get your word out and see your vision if the funding happens. Do not wait until you see whether the funding comes; do what you can before you receive the funding, so you are prepared.

Do you comprehend crowdfunding? -- Do your rescarch before embarking on this journey to understand all the different crowdfunding options available to your business. Some may be more suitable than others. Recall reading and understanding the service conditions of any crowdsourcing company you use.

Can you present yourself well? -- If you are not good at giving presentations, you may wish to hire someone to assist you so that you can show all you can do and do to the best of your possibilities to potential donors, backers or investors.

Also, please remember that only around 1/3 of crowdfunding for businesses achieves their fund goals. In some cases, this means that they will not receive any funding at all. But that really doesn't mean it doesn't mean trying is a smart idea.

TYPES OF CROWDFUNDING

Types of Crowdfunding

Crowdfunding is basically where the idea of raising capital begins. This can be money you need for a special project, a new startup, a charity, a medical service, or even a vacation that you want to spend. You can set up a crowdfunding account to raise funds for practically everything.

Some companies (and individuals), using this simple method, have been saved from financial ruin.

And like the Lone Ranger who rides and saves the day, this method also helps save many from the jaws of financial disaster.

Traditional Loan

As it became harder and harder to get the normal kind of traditional loans, in part because of the dot com bubble that burst a few years ago, this way of raising funds saved many new startups from the wall.

3 Great crowdfunding features

There are three excellent reasons why you should find this method of collecting funds for your project:

1. Companies and individuals don't have to pay back the funds because they don't receive loans but donations.
2. The real funding is spread among hundreds of small to medium-sized companies, and no one company loses a significant sum of funds.
3. Contrary to the standard way of investing, you will not have to place part or all of your company on collateral, so that your company is always under control.

Draw Win-Win

Crowdfunding gives all those looking for funding and potential donors a win-win scenario. The owner of the project will receive its funds, while the investors are rewarded according to the scenario of the financing proposal.

Points to be considered

You can start a fundraising campaign in several ways, you can choose one of the many online sites available to set up a campaign, or you can find your own crowdfunding software and build your own site.

You have to know that most sites offering these services need you to reach your main goal; otherwise, you won't receive any money. They also have various charges for taking a percentage of your donations.

The main advantage of using your own crowdfunding software is that you can sometimes set up a site within minutes using the right software. This kind of software is not all that popular, but some places allow you to use the software to set up your own fundraiser websites but also to set up consumer websites for the software price.

Your Pick

The important thing to consider right now is whether you choose one of the many crowdfunding websites available or whether you are going to use the less costly route to get your own software and set up your own crowdfunding site.

How Crowdfunding Helps Startups

"Success is best if it is shared." We also hear people thanking somebody for the achievement they have accomplished, be it friends, mentors, or wives. Have you ever heard that someone thanks to the crowd for its success?

The first thought that comes to mind when you think about starting your own business is funding. Personal savings, loans made by friends, family members, and bank loans are the most common ways to finance the startup, and an entrepreneur could pitch Venture Capital companies or the Angel Investor for funding through a detailed business plan. With the change in time and technology, Crowdfunding now offers an alternative source of funding for startups.

Crowdfunding is an alternative way to raise money from a large number of people via the internet if you are not familiar with this concept. You simply have to prepare and upload a campaign on a crowdfunding website and make it viral using social media. People who really know about the idea and are invested in it would succeed. In return, they will earn a salary or property.

Since there are various crowdfunding forms, two of them are ideally suited for startups:

1. Reward-based Crowdfunding – The backers will receive a reward for their contribution under this type of Crowdfunding. This prize may be a handwritten note or a quick bird's personalized gift. It shows the owner's gratitude to the backer, and these are the things money can't buy and gives the backer a special feeling.

2. Crowdfunding equity-based – people who contribute to your campaign will be rewarded with the company's equity/shares.

With this unorthodox funding strategy, entrepreneurs' financial challenges are diminishing. They don't need to knock the investors' door, pitch, and persuade them until the very end. You don't have to be frenetic and send lectures to others. All you need to do is show your business online.

Crowdfunding makes it possible for companies, rather than just individual donors, to carry their innovations to a wider audience. Through today's social media, it is much easier to find like-minded people to add to the idea. Anyone can contribute to your idea; just make sure people know your project.

So, if you have a finance proposal, brace yourself to make it work! Get funded! Get crowdfunded!

Crowdfunding: How Your Nonprofit Can Get Started

If your organization is interested in raising money in the crowdfunding area, these are some tips and strategies to remember:

* Many crowdfunding sites are available, but some of them are Kickstarter, IndieGoGo, CrowdRise, and FirstGiving. When considering which platforms to use, consider carefully how a campaign would work within a particular site, specifically with respect to fees, transaction costs and whether or not you need to achieve your financial goals in order to obtain any funds raised.

* Imagine Crowdfunding as either a microfundraiser. Therefore, the best successful campaigns are for a specific project, initiative, or activity, where you have time to raise money. Crowdfunding should not be used in practice to raise general dollars.

* The first 30 percent is a good rule to use once you start a crowdfunding campaign within the first 48 hours.

* Make sure that you first promote the campaign in your own donor base. Non-profit often tend to get the wrong impression that a good

crowdfunding campaign should take place when new donors are going to donate the money. Yeah, a good campaign includes new contributors, but who you meet starts also, and encourages them not just to join their efforts but to help spread the message.

* Keep in mind that your supporters are the best advocates and ambassadors. Consider Crowdfunding always in the context with your own general fundraising efforts. In order to effectively finance this form of financing, it should be used as one revenue source to raise certain revenue sources for a specific initiative or program. When you organize a campaign, you can help the company tell a compelling story.

* Ensure it's intimate. For decades, the best marketers know that telling a story is the best way to "sell." When you promote your crowdfunding campaign, people not only have to understand the facts but to involve them, and they also need to appeal to their emotions. Telling your personal stories on how this campaign affects someone's life will help you connect with donors as well as prospective donors.

* If you are in the middle of a crowdfunding campaign, dynamism is all. Make it a point to share with your supporters your success and progress with a variety of communication techniques (e.g., newsletters, e-mail, social media).

Non-profits use crowdfunding campaigns more and more. If the organization is new to this type of fundraising, contact other successful charities and ask them to give you their advice and tips on what works. Ask them what they have learned and what they could not do as they had hoped or will improve them in future campaigns. Peer-to-peer talks are a perfect way for non-profit organizations to learn about people in the trenches.

How to Craft a Successful Crowdfunding Pitch

Running a startup is the same as conducting and leading an orchestra simultaneously in order to maximize performance. Mike Shapiro, founding and CEO of The Alternative Press, operates a high-growth company that falls between a typical main street business and a Google or AOL company. How they end up on the scale of potential is yet to be seen and relies potentially on their willingness in the future to collect money.

After $100,000 in the investment of his own money and two years' wages forgotten, it was time for major expansion. "A designer sporting lots of hats just gets you so far," Mike says. In contrast to many companies now in their life-cycle, Mike's business is earning positive revenues, which means that they pay all their bills on income and have a little to spare. To several (if not most), holding the light on typically drives a company to collect money for investment.

The Alternative Press is an online, local news company that sells licenses to local businessmen, who run their own local news business as long as the corporate parent's infrastructure. After testing the licensing model in 10 markets, the next natural step was to scale the business in more than 100 markets. This would require $1 million to raise money ideally. Mike worried that repaying his loan would restrict investment in critical areas, such as sales, marketing, and infrastructure, even if the company were qualified for a bank loan. Alternatively, he wanted to allow qualified investors – people who meet certain wealth and annual income criteria – to spend some of their capital for equity in his business.

There are two options: angel investors or risk capitalists. During the first round of fundraising, Angel investors are more balanced, as risk entrepreneurs spend just 3 percent of their funds during early-stage firms (as against later startups attracting the bulk of VC financing). Individual investments in Angel tend to be smaller, requiring more of them to complete the fundraising process, but returns can be significant. Nick Hanauer, for instance, a businessman from Seattle, invested $40,000 on Amazon.com-at one point; his purchase was valued at $250 million.

Mike has chosen to pursue angel investors through a private investment known as a REG D 504 offer. It could also create an AngelList campaign or a Gust campaign, two popular web-based platforms where angel investors can assess numerous opportunities for investment. The Securities and Exchange Commission will also be an option once the rules for the JOBS Act are concluded.

Mike has partnered with a corporate attorney, a bookkeeper, and his current Boss, Jim Lonergan, who was a career businessman, having operated popular media businesses like TheStreet.com. He developed a marketing plan, a presentation deck, and a proposal document in consultation with these advisers. He is now working with his network to identify and meet accredited investors in the hope of writing a check.

Several key points fall into the pitch:

* A consumer trend to find both "hyper-local" and online content in order to manage daily living

* The local online ad market is immense and growing ($15 trillion), with more and more advertisers moving their budgets to targeted local advertising.

* Proven and attractive business model in 10 current markets able to achieve 40% + margin

The target is one million dollars, and 20% of the equity is given in return. Investments can be as small as 25,000 dollars and as large as 1 million dollars. "It's never easy to ask for the money," he says. "I 'd prefer to be asking for the business. However, every day, we see the success of the business, a new licensee coming in, a new advertiser committing $15,000 to an annual advertisement expenditure, we continue building trust in the business and in the business model, and so the raising gets easier."

* Many individuals, although financially eligible, are not very interested in private investment, and the opportunity requires time to digest it.

* The business model/financials will be spoken about, reached, and accepted so creditors would make more confident decisions than they have previously believed.

So far, Mike and The Alternative Press have verbal commitments for $250,000, and they look forward to the end of the first half of this fundraising round. Mike estimates that about 25 percent of his time is spent gathering funds and constantly enhances his pitch for every meeting while listening closely to investor queries.

PLATFORMS FOR CROWDFUNDING

Platforms for Crowdfunding

With startup seed capital hard to find every day, many businesses are looking at crowdfunding platforms to increase their startup funding.

What does crowdfunding mean? It represents the collaborative actions of individuals who network and pool their money, usually over the Internet, to help others or organizations make efforts. Crowd financing is used to support a wide variety of activities, including disaster relief, public journalism, fan artists' support, policy campaigns, startup corporate funding, film or free software development, and research.

Fred Wilson, the founder of neon Square Ventures venture capital firm (which has invested in Tumblr, Twitter, Zynga, and Foursquare), forecasts that the shareholding crowdfunding market would reach 300 billion dollars once the crowdfunding scenario gets up and running, driven mainly by family and individuals investing a small percentage of their assets over crowdfunding. Research by Crowdsourcing.org found that nearly $1.5 billion by 452 crowdfunding sites were collected in 2011.

Below is a list of the best crowdfunding sites to check for if you are a startup businessman.

Kickstarter: The oldest and strongest crowdfunding platform is probably Kickstarter. Kickstarter has a success rate of 44%, with over 74 projects launched on its website and $383 million raised on its website for projects. It helps to finance everything from movies, games, music, art, design, and technology. Kickstarter is filled with ambitious, innovative, and imaginative projects, which are implemented directly by other people.

WeFunder: Wefunder is a plethora of startup founders. They help seed investors to buy stock in the most promising new businesses around the country for as little as $100. The founders also help fund their most passionate users who offer product feedback, marketing evangelism, and business connection. The company was founded by the MIT Sloan School of Management in January 2010. As written on its site, it now boasts an enormous number of investments: 9,287 founders pledge to invest $25,989,550 in startups

Indigogo: Indiegogo is one of the largest and earliest websites in the world for crowdfunding. They also helped raise millions of dollars across 194 countries through more than 30,000 campaigns. Each of Danae, Eric, and Slava tried to raise money for what they cherished, but they were unsuccessful. They had good ideas, a passion for hard work, and good networks, but their access to funding via traditional channels was limited. The trio was determined to solve the problem. Indiegogo was born, a crowdfunding solution that enables people to easily donate their ideas.

Crowdfunding: Crowdfunder in Los Angeles is a social network for business people and investors to connect, crowdfund, and grow. The company provides tools, links, and advice to business owners and investors at every stage of the company's life cycle. Small companies and startups can raise funds using equity, debt, and contribution-based instruments. Crowdfunder also runs a variety of events in cities across the United States that deal with local companies that have the potential to obtain funds up to $ 500,000. However, this website focuses mainly on the US market.

RocketHub: RocketHub is a digital practitioner crowdfunding site. On this platform, there are project topics with various tag words from stunning to strange. Rockethub has recently gained a lot of popularity due to its continuous exposure to the media.

SeedInvest: A website focused on American startups and created by a group of MBA professionals from the Wharton School at the University of Pennsylvania. SeedInvest brings entrepreneurs and investors together in a way that was never before done via an equity-based crowdfunding platform. SeedInvest enables entrepreneurs to reach millions of investors across the US to raise seed capital.

Quirky: Quirky is an inventor crowdfunding website. For centuries it was a tough gig to become an "inventor." Complexities regarding finance, engineering, distribution, and legalities have hindered brilliant people's ideas. Quirky has rapidly changed the way the world thinks about product development since its launch in 2009.

Startsomegood: Startsomegood is a social entrepreneurs' crowdfunding website. Start Any Change is a modern crowdfunding website to collect funds through a group of supporters. On this website, you can even see a project from India.

Fundable: Funded by Wil Schroter, a serial entrepreneur, fundable investors have an opportunity to invest for equity in small businesses. The website now operates a reward-based funding platform.

Believers Fund: This website is intended for mobile applications. This groundbreaking crowdfunding site collaborated with businesses such as Microsoft Bizspark and became a crowdfunding hub.

Fundamentals of Crowdfunding

Crowdfunding is, by definition, a way of financing a company by increasing financial contributions from many people. It is mainly achieved by using the Internet via websites that permit businesses to raise money; the concept can also be implemented by other means.

Recently, Crowdfunding has become a trend in business, whether it is a start-up or a successful business. Massolution, a consulting company headquartered in the United States, has estimated that businesses have earned billions of dollars from over 600 crowdfunding sites worldwide. It is undoubtedly a major new source of funds for innovative new enterprises, non-profits looking for contributions, and artists seeking recognition for their creative efforts.

Kickstarter, Indiegogo, LendingClub, and Fundable are some of the numerous crowdfunding platforms available. Donations are sought on these platforms in exchange for special compensation. Although each website has its own special words, all websites share the same overarching definition.

Crowdfunding also allows loans and royalty funding to be collected. For instance, the LendingClub site enables the members to directly invest in and borrow from each other and removes the banking intermediary in the transaction. The idea is to bring together entrepreneurs and investors. It is also planned to sell business stock or stakes inequity on crowdfunding web pages as well as an initial, unlimited public bid.

What makes crowdfunds worthy is that it offers start-ups or companies at the early stage to launch a product or service without exposing the entrepreneur to investors or loan officers' whims and whims. Furthermore, a successful crowdfunding campaign not only provides a business with necessary cash but also creates a base of customers that believe that they have a role to play in the business.

Crowdfunding certainly has an enormous advantage for a starter, but it's not without its own advantages. For e.g., if the campaign is not well organized, it will be a massive waste of time. It could be even worse if you achieve your objective but then realize how much money you needed. Your reputation is not only at risk here; consumers will even sue a corporation if their commitment is not kept.

Another thing is that if a company is funded by a bank or an investor, they provide business mentoring to entrepreneurs, but miss such mentoring when they choose to fund Crowdfunding.

The following features can ensure a successful crowdfunding campaign.

Reach a set of friends, families, and friends who share your passion for business and are prepared to help launch this campaign and encourage others to give.

Take a compelling business plan and explain how money can support your company.

Raise your level of gravity by showing the people how much you have invested personal funds in the company as a business person.

If you offer rewards in exchange for money, make sure the rewards are worth it. Avoid t-shirts if you're not in the category of clothing.

Crowdfunding Your Way to Financing

You have a great idea. Or to fund an artsy project such as the re-corporation of a ska album, the publication of alternative lifestyle magazines, or a film festival of the 1980s. Perhaps the project at the film festival can wait. The point is that you could be an entrepreneur, an artist, or just a regular person with a great idea, and you cannot get it off the ground because you have no funding.

You used to depend on three Fs, friends, family, and family friends. It's not always a good idea to ask all your friends and relatives for money for too many reasons to get into it. Even if you agree to repay any money, the added cost will not be worth it in the long run.

Enter Crowdfunding, which is yet another way to get the "crowd" or the three F's and a new S, strangers. You are posting your project on one of the world's more than 450 public financing platforms and waiting for the money to roll in.

In the United States and Canada, there are three kinds of crowdfunding activities that are legal. Reward-oriented or use of benefits is one kind of Crowdfunding to help sponsors. For instance, you would give some advantages i.e., a free t-shirt, free video game version, etc ... Then you have donations that mean that if someone likes your idea sufficiently, they only give you money.

The third type is Crowdfunding based on the loans that you just borrow.

Foreigners' money. Shares-based investing in the U.S. or Canada is not currently legal because it requires the sale and declaration of shares and will entail approval from the Stock Exchange Commission and Canadian regional stock commissions.

In the USA, President Obama signed the JOBS Act, which outlines the specific rules of equity financing on 5 April 2012. The SEC has 270 days from the date of implementation to set down clear guidelines and procedures and ensure that funding takes place effectively. So in the next six months, we will find out exactly how the rules apply.

But that's not why this post is being read. You want to know how to raise money by Crowdfunding. This is where your thousands of Facebook and Twitter friends will be helpful. You ought to tell everyone about your campaign and tell them every time you raise some money. Don't forget that they have a personal network that can contribute to your project.

Post a publicity communiqué and give it to magazines and blogs you know your story is involved in. You always want an interesting story, so make sure it is yours!

You shouldn't forget to explain to donors how you can spend their money in exchange.

Anatomy of a Startup: Raising Money

Although crowdfunding has been around for a while, it has become a daily term only quite recently. Currently, there are many different websites and choices for crowdfunding platforms, and many new startups and entrepreneurs can finance their ideas and projects worldwide.

Crowdfunding is a very special and very different means of collecting money for the ventures than finding financing using more conventional approaches. Firstly, you try to get a completely disparate public to impress: instead of businessmen concerned solely with the facts and figures, you appeal to your exact audience for support and financing.

As you try to call on your audience for this idea or project, you need to think about your crowdfunding in a completely different way to the traditional collection of funds. And the call for support from an audience is almost entirely based on marketing strategy.

Crowdfunding = commercialization

Once you launch your crowdfunding project, a lot of preparation is required. You need to plan your idea and get the project ready as soon as your target funding is reached. This means that all your design, team and strategy have to be in place before you start crowdfunding.

However, you must start attracting an audience and fan base while you design and plan your project. It is important that an appropriate role is established in social media so that as many people as possible can communicate. Build a solid fan base and support on your social media platforms if you haven't, as these are your major contributors.

In addition to providing a solid foundation for social media fans and consumers, it is important to build a strong marketing strategy. You need to let people know before you even begin your crowdfunding project. Call on the areas you feel your audience is going to be and try to get excited about your next project. Warn people about it! Tell people about it!

Remember, your crowd funders are your audience. And once you get them to support and finance your idea, they will be your first consumers after the project is completed. You will need a genius marketing campaign historically, and it is crucial to get this underway long before the company was produced even through crowdfunding. Also, it is vital to maintain this audience communication, especially on social media, when you have finished crowdfunding-use it to keep your funders up to date with the progress of the project and when they can finally get hold of it.

Your plan for business

You can only begin to plan your crowdfunding strategy after creating a marketing strategy and attracting interest and an audience that is excited about the project.

First of all, you must consider the crowdfunding method as a business plan. Find out how much money you have to raise and make a minimal amount of money that will affect your project. Develop a deadline to ensure that your financing keeps track and motivates your funders. It is important to plan how your crowdfunds are used-including the precise reasons behind your fund objective.

It is helpful for your public to be honest and transparent: explain precisely how your project works and why you need the money. It is important that the project is clearly split together and how funds are used, even if your crowd funders and supporters may not necessarily focus on these facts and figures.

Respond to all questions

When you create your crowdfunding pitch, you have certain main questions to answer. Then build your pitch around these questions:

1 – Who are you, and what is your background?

2-Why must I trust my money to you?

3 – What's this project?

4-Why is this particular idea? / What is the only point of sale?

5-How much money do the crowdfund need?

6-How is it going to be used?

7 – How long is the project going to take after crowdfunding?

8 – Are there any rewards or incentives, and what are they?

9-How do you maintain interaction and notify your participants during and during the creation of the project?

This is also the time to answer your own questions: study the various websites and channels for crowdfunding to figure out which one is right for you. Recall reading the fine print in detail and knowing all facets of your chosen site.

Write a pledging presentation.

Once you've created this crowdfunding, it's time to get innovative. The point of the presentation is that you have to reach your target audience and cater to them. You want to catch the interest of the funders in the header and the first few lines to build a spot that really stands out.

Concentrate initially on the plot. Describe how you came to the concept and the story behind the dream. Make the story enticing and plot, describe the background story, and any challenges you have faced before actually developing the idea. Humor is optional but can add an additional appeal, depending on the nature of the project.

The pitch must be distinguished. Using titles, bold callouts as well as interesting points on the website to break up those large text explanations. You can also make your text fascinating by using photos, pictures, video clips, graphs, or other similar forms of photos to interrupt your text and using user-friendly, clear, concise text to correctly translate your comments.

Audio & Visual Commitment

You may want to think about a video after your written piece is perfected. A video is a very helpful and beneficial way to get support, and people often enjoy watching a video about your project instead of reading the text.

The video will be about 3 minutes long and not any longer. In addition, within or after the first 10 seconds, your audience must be involved, although the pitch allows you to insert many videos instead of just one. You can use video snippets to support your points in the entire text or simply make a pitch more interesting.

If you don't want a video to be created, you should use pictures. Creates an interesting, engaging, and relevant header image and preferably more pictures. At least some fascinating images are always on the best pitches, and your prospective idea or project must be visually shown at least once.

Now you have your crowdfunding pitch, written and visually interesting, that should attract and draw people in. You just need to practice and be sure it's perfect: practice with your friends and family and receive honest feedback-if they didn't know you, would they donate it?

Ask how else you can get assistance with your proposal. Will people encourage you and promote the plan in many ways? Encourage the writers to talk and encourage them entirely.

So, you're going there! You will be able now to write down your good and dedicated crowdfunding presentation.

If you need any assistance to promote your crowdfunding project and to implement a tailored marketing and social media strategy, we can help you!

Crowdfunding Campaign

Today, crowdfunding is becoming more popular. Indeed, the battle for page views and pledges is becoming more and more competitive, particularly on portals that include multiple live projects simultaneously. For firms looking for tips on how to optimize their crowdfunding campaign for success, you know that techniques and secrets are the best way to achieve your objectives.

You have to be aware of different crowdfunding secrets.

Social Media Strategy -Experts have highlighted that you would not require a full social media presence. You have to choose the networks that best suit the communication and advertising plans and identify potential supporters. You shouldn't forget to adapt your promotion to suit every platform.

Get an excellent video-visitors will have a much better idea of the project with video clips. Videos will enable your customers to view you or your offers rather than just clicking a series of static pictures. However, remember that an amateur-looking video isn't enough to persuade anyone to participate. Indeed, this can even damage your campaign 's credibility. That said, it is a worthwhile investment that you get expert help to make the video pitch it is best it could be.

Produce a useful media page – The press often features popular crowdfunding projects. This will not happen unless you have a solid website and also some press materials which are easily downloaded by many journalists. Know that you must not rely solely on your Facebook page even when you're a one-man show. Bear in mind that journalists may choose to promote other projects if they can't seek more information about your project.

Communicate always-Whether it's good or bad, and you always have to keep your supporters in a loop. Consider posting regularly on your crowdfunding page and remember to continue the process after the campaign has ended.

Keep it real – You have to present your squad so that your followers know the people behind the initiative even when you're either an existing company or maybe a start-up. The attitude and style must be considered in the crowdfunding campaign.

Creating a compensation scheme-it is indeed an intelligent strategy. Researchers suggest you have to talk about designing a reward scheme at varying price points.

Be aware that there is no precise way of guaranteeing crowd success. However, you are definitely able to maximize your chances by studying strategies, projects, and secrets already working for others.

You Created a Crowdfunding Campaign, Now What?

One of the greatest mistakes people make about crowdfunding is expecting people to visit their crowdfunding page automatically when it is created. In the end, crowdfunding platforms are simply creating the infrastructure needed to efficiently collect funds online, and you still have to market your crowdfunding campaign to mobilize donors.

So how do you market a single crowdfunding page to maximize the results of fundraising? I describe ten ways to maximize your crowdfunding experience.

1. Say a story

All loves a good narrative that is interesting for a good story. Don't just tell donors why donations are needed. Tell them the story behind what led you to start your effort. Consider building a blog to expand your story beyond the views of donors on your crowdfunding page. This is particularly important if you have photographs of past experiences related to your cause or documenting ongoing funding activities and events.

2. Drive back social media

Twitter and Facebook are generally the most effective social media platforms for shifting your fundraising page. The creation of fundraising graphics is particularly effective for your organization and supporters to share in social media. The long these graphics are displayed, and the more people they display, the greater the impact (setting the graphics as profile photos or cover pictures is a great idea).

Furthermore, it is a common practice to create Facebook groups or events to publicize individual crowdfunding campaigns. If you want to go this way, setting a similar fundraising target on behalf of the case (Help Joe collect $1000 for hurricane relief) invites people to help you reach a concrete purpose. Ensure that all social media posts and any graphics your organization creates include a link to your crowdfunding campaign. Finally, don't just post once and expect huge results, communicate frequently and regularly with potential supporters!

3. Start a $1.00 Campaign

In today's social media age, every member of your organization, if not thousands, has hundreds of contacts that they can immediately access. Imagine the impact if everyone gave just $1 to your campaign. A quick and efficient fundraising strategy can be just that: requesting ten contacts from each member of your organization, for a minimum donation amount. In general, people are much more receptive than a general request for an unnamed sum to a request for a small and specific donation.

4. Incentives offer

Whether you are a college student or an established business, donors can easily be rewarded with a certain level of donation. These may be theater tickets, gift baskets, etc., but the best rewards for your fundraising cause are relevant. Incentives don't even have to be expensive, anything that is as basic as a signed photograph can be a personal and economic reward.

5. Ask the donors

All the fundraising work is easy to attribute to the online community, but don't rely on intimate connections with your relatives, colleagues, and peers. Before leaving the door every morning, put some of the cards with the link on your crowdfunding page. So, whenever you talk about your cause (which, I hope, often happens), it's easy to raise your funds and give the person a card.

6. Audio Video

Videos are one of the easiest places to illustrate a campaign and to attract supporters. Most people are put away by this concept because they think it is time and money to film a video, especially if they run individual crowdfunding projects with little resources. But new apps for phones and tablets have greatly simplified the process of creating a video. Many not familiar with the recording process should try out stop motion camera applications (e.g., iMotion HD), which are a short and easy way to make a professional video. No matter what direction you want to go, remember to include the connection to your crowdfunding website, preferably at the start and at the end.

7. Receive news attention

Local papers and university student publications are often open to articles about individuals and/or organizations that have a positive impact or are trying to achieve an objective for a good cause. If a newspaper is eager to discuss your story, ensure that you have the background behind your fundraising activities, and invite the reader to enter your crowdfunding group. Don't know where to start? Do not know where to start? A fast search by Google for local publications and their contact details is a successful start. Many newspapers do provide material on their blogs for interested guest contributors.

8. Mobilize networks in your network

Somebody you or your company meets has its own website, forum, or internet presence. Some may even have access to the websites of other organizations. Find out who these people are and ask them if they are prepared to display the crowdfunding platform on their website. If you find people with website content that are relevant to your cause, this strategy has the greatest chance of success.

9. Place a Quantitative Concept

At the end of the fundraising effort, this technique is extremely successful. It is time to make one more major move as you hit your target. Let your supporters know just how close you are to your goal and how much time it takes ("Only 50 dollars away from our 1500 dollars and four days to go!"). With the pressure of an imminent deadline, fans can pitch in the last bit and pull you across the stretch.

10. Start

It is important to keep track of all your supporters and thank them for donating to your cause after your fundraiser campaign ends. This not only lets you know that you are respected, but it also allows you to support your future crowdfunding activities. A personal thank you card is ideal for smaller donor bases; thank you, emails can be more useful for large donor bases. Finally, it is good practice to let the donors know how they were doing the initiative they supported (photos are a plus) to see how their money worked.

Important Things You Must Know Before Commencing A Crowdfunding Campaign

You need to learn a few important things if you are thinking of starting a crowdfunding venture. Experts say that before you do, you should read this guide to avoid the usual crowdfunding pitfalls.

Your Crowdfunding Guide

Determine whether crowdfunding is right for you – you should not underestimate the financial and human resource costs of these efforts. Please remember that you won't get free money. There is a lot of work to be done, and you expect to invest a considerable amount of your money and time to create a successful campaign. In addition, consider not using this as a last resort. If you run out of money, don't have sponsors, or maybe are in a high-risk industry, it's wise not to spend the last few cents out of the crowd.

Plan-What to expect and what reaction the campaign might receive is very hard to determine. If you are among those lucky people with viral campaigns, you must be willing to attend the Internet, answer telephones, and support your growing community. So you have to prepare every day and make sure you have dedicated people who run the campaign once it is online. Be aware that the work has not yet been done after your campaign has started.

Use the right platform-different platforms that are accessible from which you can select. Please take some time to understand everyone so that you can choose what is right for you. There are several inquiries you should, therefore, ask yourself before you commit to a certain platform. Ideally, you must choose a platform that will suit your project together with the industry in which you work.

Get legal help-After knowing that what platform is right for you, you have to be very careful. This is very important to ensure that you are not liable to pay the money back later. Legal assistance will ensure you won't be surprised in the future. Conduct research now gets all the necessary help from pros, and save oneself from potential crises along the way.

Learn how to build trust, and transparency-people will surely finance the product if they like it. Be aware that it is crucial for a successful campaign to be transparent and to create trust with the crowd. Also, if something looks sketchy, people will give their money less likely.

Crowdfunding Tips for Non-Profits

Here are some things to remember for the crowdfunded campaigns

Don't be optimistic— the level of exposure which the power of the Internet carries with it can easily overwhelm you. Set realistic goals. Not every view of your page translates into donations. It's all right. It's all right. Trust and inspire your network to support your initiative. All will come, and you'll find the donors.

Work on the content-Most of the time, undecided visitors can be converted to ready donors. Undertaken projects, success stories, vision, action plan, mission all demonstrate clear thinking that generates confidence throughout the campaign. Use videos and photos to add your content dimension. After all, donors want to learn how to use their hard-earned money.

Using technology — The technology could even make things easy for you, whether it's promoting the campaign, organizing the content, staying connected to the donors.

In contrast to the common belief, the packaging is nearly as important as content. Even willing donors would also eventually give up when the website is heavy/hard and navigating.

Keep the donors in the loop, finally. Express gratitude after the donations have been received. Keep them fresh. Keep them updated. Inform them how much your money was good for you. All this would inspire them to give more to the cause.

Engagement by volunteers or backers

Volunteers are like cogs for your crowdfunding equipment. The most common mistake made by the campaign organizers in this area is not to pay sufficient attention to voluntary needs. The campaign owner should realize that the involvement of these well-wishers as well as supporters in the first level network, the strength of which is their friends, relatives, and colleagues to promote the campaign to its success.

From the first contact to coordination in an ongoing campaign, clearly define roles and how the contribution of all is important (in terms of resource or time). It gives the volunteers a sense of entitlement as well as achievement, and you set the stage for your campaign from day one. Experts say a good start helps to attract more attention and numbers. Set the targets for the day, contact the team. The capacity to be viral across networks in the first few days is greatest.

Don't forget about the recompenses. In cases of charity, expressing gratitude and a vote of thanks is always more important than cash rewards. This goes above the usual costs that volunteers pay over the lifespan of the case. Volunteers cannot be expected to pay for travel or food or provisions. If that is the case, it should communicate clearly from the very beginning.

It is critical that all stakeholders fulfill their needs. Collect your supporters' feedback. It will not only help you with future events but also helps you to match your volunteer interests with the events you plan to organize.

While a number of other things affect the success of a campaign, most of them are campaign-specific. The above points can be very basic crowdfunding guidelines, but it is up to you to continue to improve, to improve, and to continue delivering.

Crowdfunding is a way to support a cause through different Internet channels, including the general public. A crowdfunding campaign requires a lot of communication and energy, particularly if the collection goal is high.

Raising Capital with Crowdfunding

Crowdfunding is not new, but many of you just start to hear about it and how you can use it to raise money for almost anything. While it seems, you can just launch a campaign on Kickstarter or some other platform and then watch the cash roll in, it's not so easy.

You wouldn't start a crowdfunding campaign if you didn't want it to succeed, right? So, what are the main aspects of a successful crowdfunding campaign?

To begin with, make sure you have reflected on your plan, ask yourself questions such as:

- Do I have a clear picture, and can I clearly communicate that idea?
- Am I sufficiently excited with my vision to convince others "to join my cause?"

- How am I going to reward my supporters? What can I offer to encourage them to give?
- What are my ways to get the message out?

I want to warn you equally. It's not as easy as crowdfunding could be. If you only take a look and start asking for donations, you won't find anyone to give money to your campaign. It takes time to build and train the audience. How are you going to meet them, and what kind of bonuses will appeal? Think of these things before you launch your donation page.

After that, you have work to keep in touch with your audience and increase your interest in your campaign and then reward your supporters after your campaign has ended.

Despite all the effort, however, crowdfunding is an innovative way to finance a wide range of things. For example, crowdfunding has been used to collect money for a business, to promote a new product, to check the market and see if the project became a good seller, and pay before a novel, movie, screenplay, or game is written, the list goes on and on.

Look at certain crowdfunding sites like Kickstarter or Indegogo, and you can see people financing everything from child insurance to family holidays. If you can imagine something and communicate it clearly to people behind your idea, it could be funded. Now it's your turn, have you an idea, cause, or need that could be financed by crowdfunding?

CREATING AN AUDIENCE (CROWDFUNDING AUDIENCE)

The Perfect Audience

One of the challenges facing most speakers is to engage or engage the audience. It wouldn't be good to have a reactionary crowd. The speaker is moved into action with all his enthusiasm and excitement to inspire the audience to speak and has a timer built into the mentee, waiting to trigger the audience.

It would only be too late and unfortunate to realize from the moment that the presenter asks for people participation and that he comes to the harsh awakening that the desired outcome is not achieved, which could crush or cause him or her to make further mistakes, creating an atmosphere not so promising and an uneventful presentation.

We can avoid these situations, my brothers and sisters. Let me inspire ideas that could alter the course of your presentation, making it not only interactive but also interesting.

Construct bridges

You can make as many people as possible before your voice, or when you speak, praise the crowd, or finally get a certain favorite or some followers. Just make friends so that you don't talk to a cold audience.

Observe member bodies

Look for possible gestures and motions of your audience and pay close attention to those who are nodding for acceptance or smiling and building on them, and they are your anchors that shed light on your environment.

Be a Teller of Story

Stories are always fantastic, but if they were your story, people are more engaged and personalized to make it powerful. It allows people to talk to you and to share it with you. Barrier walls would come down. It would inject some witty mood or even ask the audience what they think the moral of the story was or even better let it go.

The game's play

Everyone I know is fond of participating in a game. Playing a game makes it possible to produce creative judges, revive our infancy and relax. You will be rewarded with the floodgates of an appreciated crowd when you show the audience or make their time beautiful. Use it as an excellent lever.

Donor of gift

Leading you to the truth, like a child with sweets, everybody loves to take something away. If they know that from their meticulous analysis, they would benefit anything that would tax them.

See it in your mind that a dynamic and engaging presentation is a mental obstacle to participation. Use these five ideas to help your audience motivate and inspire. A portion of food for thinking from E.W Howe, "If he didn't know that it was his next step, nobody would hear you talk."

How to Grab Your Audiences' Attention Instantly

As you are doing an interview with your audience, you have to make a positive impression with your audience in the shortest time possible, as a public lecturer. The opening segment of your presentation is the possibility to build relationships with the crowd, to gain attention and confidence, and to warm them up for a wonderful time with you.

The first words I hope any speaker will say will be "Good morning/afternoon/evening." Obviously, these first words will do you no wrong. So let the listeners know of the main points, then let the crowd know that the next few minutes, hours or days would be of value to them. Pick the wording wisely in order to be sure that the message would be good.

Instead of saying, "You are going to know about stress control at the end of this session," suggest, "At the end of this session, you will hear about the secrets of effective stress management."

Instead of saying, "You will learn and apply some leadership techniques by the end of this seminar," say, "At the end of the seminar, you will know that everyone can be the leader through training and the application of tried and tested techniques used by some of the great leaders in the world."

Instead of saying, "I'll show you the steps to weight loss within a couple of minutes," I'll tell you how easy it is for someone in 1 week to lose 10 kilograms! Can you know the distinction between the good and the negative examples? Those terms illustrate the use of persuasive and motivating phrases that will make the viewer more focused on you. It is basically a strategy to pick up the attention of the consumer as if you were a salesman selling a very valuable product to the client.

If you have a proven technology that can potentially help other people lose substantial weighing amounts in a single week, please do not over-sell and under-sell. On the other hand, cliché recommendations or impractical theories would turn anybody off as soon as the audience discovered that your meeting was a complete wastage of time.

Another way to get the crowd's attention is to share those surprising figures with them after you meet them.

Take the following fictional example:

"Good evening, ladies and gentlemen."

Murder, burglary, and rape are the top three crimes committed almost daily... Would you be shocked or a bit embarrassed by such a statement? I'd do it. And that's exactly the goal of making such a statement right at the start. If such shocking statistics seem to amaze the audience, you could have gotten their attention.

These methods have been tested and confirmed in person on hundreds and hundreds of times.

Did you ever listen to the term crowdsourcing? You certainly know the crowdsourcing process, even though you can't remember hearing the word before. Crowdsourcing means collecting information from the public and using it to complete a business-related task. This information is then used by collaboration or resistance in a large group of citizens. Crowdsourcing offers the business the ability to easily and yet efficiently pursue new ideas. They can leverage resources outside of the organization, but this can help to build more competitive advantages.

Crowdsourcing is especially common and easy for Internet use. For companies as well as for people, because they can easily leave their ideas or express their thoughts about the product of the company. Crowdfunding is a form of crowdfunding. "Crowdfunding—a distributed audience's online request for resources often for reward—provides an alternative way for individuals and teams to seek financial support from a distributed audience." The section reveals that traditional fund-raising methods such as the application of banks' funds transform into platforms such as "Go Fund Me."

Crowd voting is another type of Crowdsourcing. "The crowd vote is a process of crowdsourcing in which a platform only promotes or sells goods and services that are supported by most of the digital crowd." Crowd voting is a way of expressing opinion only from the community, which has an interest in a specific matter. "An example of the crowd voting is the American Idol.

My 3rd and final example of Crowdsourcing is Crowd Competition. "The easiest way to get a crowd involved is to create a contest. The sponsor or organization describes a particular problem, provides a cash reward, and asks for solutions. Contests work well when it isn't clear which combination of skills or even what technical approach will lead to the best solution for the problem.' Contest holding is similar to a test sequence in that we see some differences in the results.

Hopes that we are now better able to understand the term "crowdsourcing" and understand there is a difference between at least different forms of Crowdsourcing. On a personal note of all types of Crowdsourcing, I think the crowdsourcing contest is one of the most effective ways of Crowdsourcing.

5 Dynamic Thoughts to Engage Your Audience

One of the challenges facing most speakers is to communicate or educate the audience. It would not be nice to have a non-responsive crowd. The speaker is energetic and eager to encourage the public to speak and has a mental timer built-in waiting for the audience to be interested. One of the many consequences that the speaker might face does not know whether the time was right or correct.

It will be too late and painful to know as the presenter asks the audience to participate and comes to the harsh realization that it will not produce the desired result. This would kill him or trigger him or her to make additional mistakes, to create an environment not so promising, and an eventless presentation.

We should stop these circumstances, my sisters and brothers. Let me send you ideas that could change the direction of your presentation and make it not just engaging but also interesting.

Build bridges

Any training you can do is make as many audience mates as you can. You may do this before your speech or during the speech, and maybe win some favoritism or some fans during your audience. Only by making friends, so you don't talk to a cold audience.

Observe speaker bodies

Look for the audience's potential expressions and actions, pay more attention to those who nodd or smile and draw on them. They are your anchors that shine your surroundings. You can probably aid in the interactive portion of your speech.

Ome a Teller of Story

Stories are always great, but if it were your story, people would be more engaged to make it powerful. By doing this, the audience can relate to you and share yourself with them. The barrier walls will come down. If possible, give the audience some witty humor or even ask what they think the moral of the story is or better let them share a similar short experience or story, encouraging participation. You could put the scene or the mood, so that you can direct your energy to the audience, making it two ways.

Please play the game.

Everyone I know loves to participate in a game. Playing a game will provide us with creative juices, relive our childhood, and let us relax. If you show the audience or let them have a great time, the flood gates of an appreciative crowd will reward you. Use it as an excellent lever.

Donor of gift

Leading you in truth, like a child with candy, everyone loves to walk away if they realize that from one's painstaking presentation, they would gain something which would charge them.

See in your mind that making a complex and stimulating presentation is a mental challenge for you to achieve participation. Use these five ideas to help motivate and inspire your audience. E.W. Howe's food for thought, "No one would hear you talking if he didn't know that was his next turn."

As you go to a job interview, you, as a public speaker, must make a positive impression on your audience in the quickest possible time. The opening section of your lecture is the opportunity to build relationships with the crowd, attract their attention, and trust and warm them up for a great time.

I believe the first words every speaker would bring out would be "good morning/afternoon/night." Certainly, these first words will not be incorrect for you. Then, let the audience know the delivery target. Tell them about your main terms. Let the crowd know that the next five minutes, the next few hours, or the following days would be helpful for them.

So instead of saying, "You will learn to manage stress at the end of this session, you will be able to learn the secrets of effective stress management," say, "by the end of this session."

Instead of saying: "You will be able to learn and apply some leadership techniques by the end of this seminar," say: "By the end of your seminar, you'll know how everyone can lead by learning and applying proven techniques that are used by some of the world's leading leaders."

Instead of saying, "In the next few minutes I'll show you the steps you need to take to lose weight, I'll tell you how easy it is for anyone to lose 10 kilograms within a week in the next couple of minutes!" Are you aware of the difference between positive and negative examples? These words demonstrate the use of persuasive, compelling language that can reel the audience's attention towards you. It is a simple way to attract the audience's interest as if you were a salesman introducing your customer with an extremely beneficial product.

If you have a tried and tested tool that can potentially help others to lose substantial weight in a week, tell so right at the beginning. On the other hand, cliché ideas or unrealistic hypotheses would only put anyone off once the public learned that the session was indeed a total waste of time.

Another way to get people's attention is to share some appalling statistics with them after you welcome them.

Take the following fictional example:

"Good afternoon, ladies and gentlemen, good afternoon."

The main three offenses almost on a regular basis, are shooting, robbery, and rape. I would. And this is precisely the purpose of making this statement at the beginning. If the audience seems surprised by such shocking statistics, then you would have succeeded in attracting your attention.

These methods have been tried and tested extensively and have been confirmed on hundreds of occasions.

GOAL SETTINGS (CROWDFUNDING GOAL)

Five Tips for Successful Crowdfunding

Many Americans dream of starting their own company, and the money they need to start is one of the main roadblocks in their way. Without a stable revenue stream, banks are not fond of lending money to new firms, and risk capital is inaccessible to the American average. But for young entrepreneurs, there is a new ray of optimism.

In recent months, Crowdfunding has received considerable attention as a method of funding new companies through the power of social networking. For those who are new to the concept, Crowdfunding is simply a way to raise funds for a project or enterprise by calling on an informal network of people to finance little chunks, usually in the form of small donations or income sharing. New crowdfunding sites emerge every day on the Internet, but if you take a glance at commercial projects that glance for financing, most rarely get close to their financial targets. While Crowdfunding has the potential to democratize risk capital, it takes planning to make it work, and follows several simple rules on success:

1. Choose the site, wisely-Not all crowdfunding sites are made the same, and as Crowdfunding is popular, many people want to be a part of this action. You want to choose a company that complies with SEC regulations, particularly Regulation D, Rule 504, that restricts yourself to collecting

money from family and friends with whom you have a "substantial and previously established relationship."

2. Take the time to make a well-developed pitch. Most crowdfunding efforts are unconscious because the business idea is vague, and therefore the pitch is not an investment opportunity but a handout. Even if you just ask for $1000 to get a freelancing company out of business, take the time to create a concise business plan with financial forecasts and marketing strategies. The pitch on the crowdfunding website is a condensed version of this plan.

3. The way Crowdfunding generally works is to declare an amount that you want to raise, and then it's everything or nothing; if you don't meet the aim, the partial amount promised is returned to investors. This causes many people to be selective about how many they like, but you have to be honest about how many you have to start successfully. Choose a funding strategy that is meaningful for your project. Would you want to collect small amounts from multiple investors or bigger sums from a smaller pool? The way you create and market your pitch should be affected by your choice.

4. Optimize non-monetary incentives – Sites such as Profounder are set up to offer an investor share of your earnings that works fine in large companies, but you probably won't have much to share if you plan to run your business alone. Focus on attractive non-monetary incentives if this is the case. For, e.g., someone wanting to start a professional photography company might provide discounts on family portrait sessions. This not only provides an attractive incentive, but it is also a way to create an initial customer list.

5. Be honest and show your personality—Crowdfunding is beautiful as it is interactive, which is one reason people engage in helping an entrepreneur begin with the emotional reward. Although it is vital to be polite in your presentation, you must always aspire to demonstrate your personality and why you enjoy your particular business idea.

Crowdfunding is also not easy, but if you invest the trouble to schedule carefully and practice your proposal, you are far more likely to finance your venture successfully. It's the first important step on the way to start your new business and achieve the American dream.

Goal Setting: A Quick Guide

Let's talk about setting goals, how you set goals, and how you ensure these goals are actually achieved.

How do you achieve goals not only for the New Year but for the entire year? How do you really make them change your mind, transform your life for the better?

Personally, I've been struggling for a long time with goals. It may be because they look easy. They look obvious; you must go there and begin to look at which goals actually work so that you can set the right, powerful goals to achieve your goal.

If you're like me, then you've got big life dreams. You know that you can do so much more. That means you've got some kind of dream. You've got some kind of dream.

How your career could be, how your business could grow, how your health could be, how the lifestyle is like. To do big stuff in all these places of your life, you need certain goals to get there.

Let's talk about how to do that and where people make mistakes with the process of setting goals, because I have made these errors, and even if I have studied this, I make those mistakes. Let's take that look.

There are many people who work tirelessly to accomplish the goal, but when they eventually meet those goals, they are not happy or able to achieve them. The main reason is that what you did is not suitable for your inner values. That should not happen to you. This should not happen. Clarification of values is an act in every area of your life that you need to perform.

Your real goals are the goals to achieve. It begins with developing the visions and values into tasks you can easily accomplish every day until you reach the main objective.

The main ability to succeed is to set goals and plan for such objectives. You can not fully utilize your potential or achieve any goal in life without mastering the ability to define objectives and develop action plans. Every major achievement involves a series of steps.

Via preparation, the main goal is a multi-task project with step-by-step information, consistent deadlines, and sub-deadlines. The good news is that you can learn and improve this ability with practice. The more you do, the happier you feel. You would then be one of the most effective and powerful.

Set your thoughts always on a sheet of paper. Sub-lists can be available with any list. Keep updating and revising your plan until you are comfortable with it. Any ability can be learned, and the planning of ability is no exception.

Over the years, several experiments have been carried out on why certain people gain success. To determine the common success denominator.

"Action-orientation" was the common denominator. Those who succeed take enormous measures. They move very quickly and always have full hands.

Every great achievement is an indication that one challenge or another has been overcome. Your ability to decide what you want is the critical determinant of your success. Then take steps to live in the face of obstacles to problems before you reach your goals.

So, if we are both able to set concrete, observable, realistic, and achievable goals, why is it difficult for a lot of people to set one. There are four reasons why I think it is difficult for people to really set goals.

You do not understand this Value.

They don't have the basic idea of setting targets for certain people, so they don't appreciate its significance. You don't see the need to set targets if you grew up in a household where nobody sets goals or even tries to accomplish them.

You did not guide us into putting goals.

People cannot set goals because they have no instructions about how to set goals. Worse yet, there are many who have wishes or dreams that they call objectives.

For example, "be happy," "take a lot of money," or "have a nice family life."

Naturally, both of us have desires and aspirations, but the purpose is very different from desire, precise, tangible, and also time-bound.

If you're like me, because before you became an adult, you didn't learn about the goals, you won't understand the significance.

YOU ARE FAILING AFRAID

The truth is that no one wants to fail. Failure is both physically and psychologically stressful and distressing. At one time or the other, we all failed. As we decide to learn from our experience to go ahead, we can 'cage' us and make us 'play it safely.' Therefore, we do not completely exploit our capacity.

You are a CRITICISM AFRAID.

These are people who feel that they will receive criticism from others by setting a goal and not achieving that goal. I have a simple solution for you if you come into this category, to ensure that your goals are confidential. You don't have to tell anybody about your goals. Let your successes and performances speak for you.

Th Importance of Goal Setting

A fast preamble:

For some, it is a relatively easy task to set personal goals, while for (many) others, it's just not the rule.' The 'secrets' of setting goals seem out of reach-thus, a whole mass of people are just bubbling through life and taking whatever life happens to throw them into it ...

There was a mistake. And that's because they haven't spent enough quality time deciding what they really want and the steps they didn't plan to achieve this wishes-they haven't set the goals to reach them where they want to be ..!

Have you?

To end the chase:

The Importance of Objectives ...

So, although you probably know all the good reasoning behind the target set already, experience tells me that you probably still ask, "why should I set objectives ...?"

The solution is very clear ... "MOTIVATION" it is ... At first, you set your vision precisely on what you want and/or want it, then you learn and understand every step (goal) that you need to achieve in order to make your vision (your final 'goal') a reality.

Goal setting is such an effective mechanism that it shouldn't be a challenge to keep on target while you work towards your goal since established goals have an intrinsic protection issue-any obstacles that could hinder the aim being accomplished can be detected and resolved easily.

By setting simple, ultra-defined goals, you will cheer and be very happy when you meet one and all, with the addition of a boost in self-confidence, as you succeed down the path as you felt originally was too difficult, or even unlikely. Success in any way always improves confidence and further enhances goal-oriented skills.

Knowing this: all successful people – whether in sports, business, politics, or even voluntary work – have an understanding of and use of the links between long-term and short-term vision and motivation-YOU CAN TOO ..!

Setting goals Tips ...

-- Set the first begun ... Your final dream, your Primary goal ... What are you doing, where and where do you want to be? Is it going to take one month, one year, five years, ten years?

-- Writing it down ...-Writing ... Exactly in-depth ...

-- Work backward from that point and work out every smaller individual objective you need on the way to your main objective.

-- Everything is in detail-" define "each goal ... Each information you know exists to accomplish that goal, flesh it out ... Time scales and timescales are included.

-- Narrower Target, DOWN Person ... Exactly in-depth ...

-- PRIORITISE-what 's the most important objective ? What is the most critical goal to accomplish first or next? Some goals may just be 'nice' instead of crucial for achieving your main goal of life, so do not waste your precious time!

-- BE REALISTIC – often the downfall of many a desired goal-setter ... Set goals that you know you will achieve that you know you have the know-how to fulfill the task, or will eventually have it.

-- If the goal was too simple to achieve, make the next more difficult to achieve.

-- Review your objectives every day-not necessarily "concrete casting" You may need to subtly change course on an odd day, or alter the specifics of specific intent in order to make sure that it is still entirely or even appropriate.

-- CRITICAL – not every goal you set can be achieved, each time, at the right time ... Don't be disheartened and don't really give up most definitely ... It's a temporary glitch, you 're human, and things are happening.

The Last Anecdote:

Fixing goals is a strong way to motivate you and set yourself on the way to the future you want, YOUR ideal future.

The goal-setting practice easily and quickly creates a 'circle' of self-confidence, competency, and/or improvement and overall fulfillment as you work through every goal and complete every step towards the end result you are looking for ... set goals and earn the rewards you are sure to receive as a result of your achievements ..!!!

Helping a Cause Through Crowdfunding

Charitable institutions start raising awareness of various social issues. It can address societal issues, environmental issues, medical issues, and more. Philanthropists were also people who are financially supportive of these charities. If those people are fully aware of the causes they endorse, they may continue to ask for assistance from other people. This can be called crowdfunding or crowdfunding.

What is it?

By definition, crowdfunding is a way to raise money by asking other people for donations. There have been no fixed donation amounts. Instead, charities set a goal they want to achieve through collective contributions. Someone or some interest group can do this. Many with famous philanthropists, such as celebrities and athletes who support their cause, will benefit from the large fan base they have. This is a perfect way to collect funds quickly, and they also surpass their target much of the time.

Effective crowdfunding tips

If you want to use crowdfunding for yourself, here are some tips to get you started just do it effectively:

· Pitch your cause effectively-You must effectively convey the message or vision to the target audience to help people support your cause. You will let them realize what you are working for and what the future needs. Make your pitch good, so people could see how the cause will affect their lives.

· Using various social networks, online-most people have a means of linking to the internet. Social networking platforms have millions of people logging into every day. You could really reach millions of people with minimal effort if you have a great viral campaign on these websites. Two birds with one stone will be hit because you will raise awareness of your campaign for charity as well as crowdsourcing.

· Have popular donors-It is good to have a known personality to support and donate to your cause in order to increase your credibility. It is easier for people to believe that your charity is legitimate and that the money you collect will go to the beneficiaries. News of the cause is often easier to go viral or to hit a wider network.

· Provide loyal supporters with rewards-you can also help your investors to enjoy your cause. You will get supporters to donate in cash to the contributors in exchange for their donations. Merchandise, like shirts, cups, and other things, can easily be produced massively with the support of your sponsors.

Good people

You can receive a lot of money from good people who believe in your cause. When many people get anything they believe in, nothing is impossible. If you show them where everyone's donations are going, you will stay with you. Make sure that you post photos or updates on your projects and extension programs so that your supporters can keep up with them.

Successfulness

Many crowdfunding projects have been successful and have been generously embraced by people. This is evidence that many good Samaritans are still left. This is a great way to restore faith in mankind in a world that looks full of trouble and a problem.

How to Do Business Through Crowdfunding

Many people dream of successful entrepreneurs. However, this goal can be achieved by a major roadblock. This roadblock is the capital or the initial funds needed to get the business started. Banks willing to offer capital can expect the company to have a good cash flow and a consistent business. New companies could find it difficult to get assistance from these banks. Venture capital can be another path, but that can only be a fantasy for individuals. Crowdfunding is the most real and creative path for emerging entrepreneurs. It is a new way to raise funds for new companies. This is done by means of a unique social networking method. In the recent past, it has begun to receive a lot of responses.

While crowdfunding has become the new, innovative funding type, it has not reached far and wide. For those who have learned from this will definitely agree that the fundraising process is really quick and clear. This is achieved by an indirect process, which encourages people to take a small sum of money hidden. It can also be referred to as donations or income sharing. One of the easiest ways to get new ideas for collecting funds is online. Various other forms of crowdfunding techniques are important to try. If you can follow certain simple rules, then you will have your targeted crowdfunding finance.

The most important rule is that you need to find the right crowdfunding platform. This is very important because not all bases are the same in terms of finance. As crowdfunding is the phenomenon today, there are many sites available online that can provide you with great information. You must, therefore, choose a company with SEC rules. Regulation D-Rule 504 is an important part of the list of regulations. This reduces the individual to family and friends while collecting money. For a certain time, you should have known the parties and had a good relationship with them.

In general, the company itself is ambiguous. The main task is, therefore, to present your project plan to the financing site. It should be demand rather than an investment opportunity with details of marketing strategies.

The next rule is to have a goal and say it at first. You are only permitted to use the funds in crowdfunding until the entire sum is mobilized. If not, you might need to refund the funds to the person from which they were borrowed. Those who are ready to finance your project and support your mission should, therefore, be convinced of your objectives. Your scheme would be good if you have a number of small money contributors or a handful with larger sums.

Crowdfunding Using Fundly

Crowdfunding is not just money-raising. It explicitly ties designers and developers to consumers and funders, where partnerships will grow. The donor gives money and an email address and other things for social fundraising. This is only the start of the relationship. Unlike conventional fundraising, it's the beginning and the end of the partnership where you get a fee. Everything is all! Everything is all!

There are several helpful places to support you with social fundraising, but let's talk about Fundly and why this forum may be a little different.

origin Origin

Dave Boyce was CEO of Fundly as a public funding forum in 2009-2010. In the autumn of 2010, Dave restarted the site as a non-profit service and as a service to all forms and dimensions of individuals. In 2013, David Hu took on the position of CEO as Fundly shifted its focus to a self-service model for the collection of funds from individuals and organizations.

Statistical data

- $34 trillion: global crowdfunding volume.
- $5.5 trillion: crowdfunding reward and donation.
- $2.5 trillion: Crowdfunding equity.
- 9 weeks: total active campaign length.
- 11 Days: Successful campaign preparation.
- $7,000: average amount raised for a successful campaign.

Before you launch a campaign

Crowdfunding is very interesting; they want to know why a project like yours will make the planet a better place? Please consider the following when creating your campaign:

- Set a clear objective.
- How important is your campaign? (Sufficient to get people to donate their money)

- Set the correct price.

- Provide the right incentives. (What's the donor in it?)

- Know and engage your crowd every day.

- Develop an email and social media campaign program.

- Make it confidential! Make it personal!

- Hard work!

Begin with Fundly

1. Check out Fundly

2. If you are a person raising money, click Facebook to start free, or sign in with an email address. Select Off your campaign if you are a non-profit group.

3. Enter your name, email address, password, and other information. Click Continue. To continue.

4. Build the Campaign:

a. Enter the campaign title.

a. Select location.

b. Enter the amount you would like to raise.

c. Enter your code. Enter your code.

e. Choose the category most related to your campaign type.

f. Click Continue. To continue.

5. Continue your campaign by completing the ten steps that follow. (My account looks like-not all measures have yet been completed).

Level 10 is Giving Levels – you can set different levels, and if you reach a level, you can get a T-shirt for your campaign.

6. Set up your fundraising page that includes:

a. Gallery of Video and Photo a. Updates & Comments Blog

c. Email warnings c. Donor safe payment collection

Fees Fees

You can create and share your online campaign free of charge. But once you start receiving donations, the fees are broken down.

Get your funds

When the campaign starts accepting online contributions, you should also apply for a withdrawal. You can also directly withdraw campaign funds to your bank account.

There is NO minimum amount to collect to maintain your funds. And payments are processed fast, usually between 24 and 48 hours after the donation.

TIMING (CROWDFUNDING TIMING)

Time to Consider Crowdsourcing

We are all aware of outsourcing, the capacity to get people to work, often abroad, that works for less and sometimes less. Yet a not-so-new phenomenon shifts the way that crowdsourcing takes place.

The aim is to take a task and break it into smaller bits so that anyone can do it in their free time easily. Consider transcribing an audio recording and or Photoshopping an image sequence. The distinction from standard outsourcing to crowdsourcing is that the contractors don't really learn and are always in the healthy oils U S of A. Think of it as an incentive package for our troubled times, but entirely private sector-based.

The concept is not that fresh but is being picked up due to certain significant patterns. First of all, there is a critical mass of people willing to do the work, and probably more people will be interested in the last year because of high unemployment. Second, the Internet-based tools that are used to manage jobs and complete tracking and crowds are constantly improving. Broadband adoption helps: most people are now not calling up, which is perfect because you are trying to work the crowd-based activities online for hours at a time. Finally, a solid record has been developed by many crowds, making it more compelling for project managers looking for employees.

Consequently, crowdsourcing is a big company. Several dozen firms help manage the masses of people that offer services, and some of them earn millions of dollars a year in payments from distributors between customer and supplier. Amazon's Turk Economics, eLance.com, and I recommend you listen to my podcast, first of all, with my collaborator Paul Gillin and Brent Frei, the publisher of one of the first crowdsourcing business studies.

Frei runs a company that supplies crowdsourcing, so seeing his self-interest is not too difficult. However, the report opened my eyes to see behind the idea the power and the promise. You will, for example, maximize your own time by farming boring activities to someone else who is willing to do so at much lower prices. Or compile a list of suppliers by searching their websites online. With a 10 dollars per hour intern, the task would have taken 12 hours or 120 dollars to complete this project. By dividing it into a crowd, Frei managed to achieve it for around $18.

I know what you're going to say now. How could you ensure the quality of multitudes? What about the management time and cost? There are ways to build redundancy and to have the results checked, and you can separate things so that your crowd can make sense through the right type of project management.

At Ease on Stage - How to Connect with the Crowd

The crowds are various animals. Their love is sometimes like a wave of warmth. The coldness, as well as animosity that they project, may sometimes freeze the meat. A lot of musicians who are decent on their instruments did not spend enough time sharpening their skills. Here are a couple of tips to help you with any crowd.

Never frown. Never frown. Carry a smile still. Regardless of what happens, you will have an aura of confidence. You should learn to relax, even if the mood of the crowd becomes tense. The last thing that people want to see on stage is a dadburn crybaby. Leave all your problems on the curb outside. Look at your stage time as an event that is magical in your personal life because it is, indeed.

If you play with a band, please ensure you don't take problems that the band could have on stage. If you can't connect as a band on stage, you can't connect with the crowd. The atmosphere a band puts off is incredible. If things are really in a groove, the crowd will take the ride. But the other way around is also accurate. When things get out of control between the band members, the audience can't wait to leave. If you want to keep a band together, you should discuss the whole aspect and lay down some basic rules. Anything of a sort never let the sun be angry inside the unit.

Just spend some time with the crowd before getting on stage and relate to those with whom you interact. Find a way to move the spotlight from the audience to just where you intend to go. Say, before you go on stage, you have met a couple from another town. You will be imaginative enough just to draw them into a friendly discussion. Shifting the attention of the crowds at will is very strong. Think about what you can do to get your attention off for seconds and ensure that when that attention returns, you give the hungry eyes a certain entertainment value.

Keep things in an attempt at all times on stage. Don't spend precious time tuning incessantly. You must be in rhythm. But everyone should be able to use its own tuner discreetly and quickly. On the stage, there will be no downtime. You should have a leader who understands how to bring the audience to a certain level of fun without relying on a particular song list. You must be flexible. Have a great time. Have fun.

How to Choose Your Event Timing System

If you help to run a running or biking event, you probably considered how to improve the efficiency of your timing methods. In small races, people with stopwatches standing on the finish line can be timing. However, for larger races, too many finishers are close together, so that all time cannot be registered and every competitor can be found.

Electronic timers are important for large events, and the machines have precise timing and fix the limitations of conventional timescales.

Electronic timing program benefits:

o Finishing times can be almost immediately available

o No failures because of challenging, multi-chute finishing areas

o No mistakes when athletes sport the wrong number o

o No "bandits" errors (runners not registered)

o No mistakes because of runners in the chutes who get out of order

o the bottom line is less crowded

Electronic timing has two popular methods: chips and the D-tag. Bicyclists, hikers, triathletes, and even skiers may use this.

CHIP

A thin, lightweight chip is worn on a shoelace or an ankle bracelet by the athlete. The chip identifies each rider on a mat placed at the race finish. More sophisticated chip timing devices are dynamically located throughout the entire race. These systems may also deter theft, account for slow start times because of packed start lines, and report accurately break times.

PROS

o Batteries are not available, and devices can be used repeatedly.

o the chip-style ankle-bracelet works well for events where footwear has to be changed.

o Timing is precise.

CONS

o at the start of the race, the racer must have the device scanned.

o at the end of the race, Racers must return it.

o Chips are missing pay a bill.

D-TAG

D-tag is a newer system consisting of a lightweight timing tag added to the race number. You then remove your race number from the D-tag and loop it around the shoelaces, where it is held by adhesive. As you pass through strategically positioned mattresses, your times are recorded.

PROS

o It is convenient; when the race is over, the marker is tossed out.

o the tag must not be scanned at the start of the race by athletes-the the tag has already been set for the user of this bib/race number. Run volunteers will then disperse run bibs quicker.

o Racers do not have to sit down and untie their shoes to remove their chip after a race.

o Timing is precise.

CONS

o Because the tag is attached through shoelaces, it's not ideal for activities where a move is required.

o Tags are not recycled, but they are not eco-friendly.

Both timing systems are extremely precise and work extremely well- particularly in comparison to manual timing. You may want to consider using a chip or a D-tag based on your race and what is important for you and your athletes.

The Concept of Crowd Funding

As the term suggests, crowd financing is essentially used to raise money simply by asking a multitude of individuals for a particular cause/project like political campaigns, disaster management, startup financing, and civic projects. This method of fundraising predominantly uses the Internet that a person who tries to raise funds for a certain cause/project creates a website on which he makes a profile for his cause and then aims to make people (mainly through social media) donate to that cause/project. Crowdfunding is not restricted to individuals, as companies also use it to raise funds by selling minimum equity amounts to different investors.

The conception is attributed to Joseph Pulitzer; a journalist who urged the American public to contribute to the Statue of Liberty through his daily newspapers in 1884; New York World, after the American Committee for the Statue of Liberty, had run out of funding to contribute to it. Since that time, the concept has been dynamic with the first online initiative of 1997 when US fans of the Marillion rock band raised around $60,000 via the Internet to allow the band to play in the United States after it could not go on tour because of a lack of money.

Crowdfunding types

- Debt crowd finance

This form of funding, also called peer lending, involves people putting their money in a project (as a form of lending) to ensure their money is recovered with interest. If the money is loaned to developing nations, however, it is generally paid back, without any interest, since the financer is happy to have done some social good.

- Crowd donation/reward support

This means that most people put their money into a project/cause simply because they have faith in it and, therefore, do not expect anything in return. This is the most common form of funding that encourages individuals to contribute any amount to a given project.

- Financing of the equity crowd

With this type of financing, individuals (primarily investors) put their money into a project or company in exchange for shares or shares in that project or venture.

Benefits of multitudes

I. Assists in validating a proposal

With crowdfunding, people are able to understand whether their cause and/or project has an impact on people or whether it is time and money wasted. You will know if you actually receive a financial contribution to your project.

ii. Project / cause exposure

Since these funds are generally provided through the Internet, it can actually help do a project known not only to prospective investors but also to potential customers and thus serve as a marketing platform.

iii. a mode of access to capital

Moreover, through crowdfunding, people can essentially get money to start a project without having to necessarily get in debt or give up any equity.

It also helps people to protect themselves from unforeseen risks, helps them get more ideas for their project/case, and is a way to market a product/service before it starts and also helps to build goodwill with potential customers.

Crowdfunding - The Social Way to Raise Funds

Anyone that uses social networks at any time can know UGC (user-created content) and multitude sourcing, thereby supplying other businesses with knowledge about their brands, reviews on goods and services, and responses to questions about potential new products. You get answers from your customer base directly, and it's a winning situation.

Many people respond to such requests for information out of brand loyalty-particularly if it's a brand they have been using for years, some may hear their voices sincerely and some out of inducing them to "complete our survey, and you will be able to receive a coupon for your favorite shop." This system of incentives or rewards is by far the most popular reason for participation, and while this model of 'something for something' is not new, a whole new platform exists where incentives combined with the level of philanthropy begin to take shape in society, and it is crowdfunding.

Crowdfunding, also known as crowd finance, equity crowdfunding, and hyper funding, started back in 1997 when band members collected funds to pay for tourism. This was even done without the knowledge of the band, and over the years, fans have financed several more band projects. Over the years, other individual projects have used this type of funding model to help launch their projects. Recently networks devoted to helping project owners locate supporters launched, including ArtistShare, which became the first site for music ventures in the early 2000s. The popular Kickstarter creative project site is restricted to residents in the United States, and recent statistics show that the site has financed over $250 million worth of projects. A similar incentive is given to New Zealand members of the nearby Pledge Me center, which uses the name 'raising Kiwi innovation.

One of the latest children on the crowdfunding block is Sportfunder, a sports-related crowdfunding platform. While it is still start-up mode, it has some high-profile friends and projects and the ability to finance projects in many countries throughout the world, and it is enviable that sports enthusiasts can contribute to the achievement of their sporting goals by offering global projects and global funds.

How is crowdfunding functioning? The majority of crowdfunding sites operate under an 'all or nothing' fundraising mechanism in which the founder of the project sets the minimum finance goal, and if this is not met, the donors do not contribute, and the project gets no funds. In fact, this model protects both parties. If the project requires $5,000 and the collection only reaches $2,000, the project owner cannot be expected to complete his project successfully with insufficient funding. In turn, the promoter will not pay for a project that does not leave.

As was eluded before, when it comes to sponsoring projects, there is a level of incentive as well as reward combined with such an element of philanthropy. Each project offers a reward for its financial contribution to the supporter. The incentives differ from project to project and differ considerably from the project, and the 'exposure' amount should be received from the sponsor. Any acknowledgment may take the form of a social note-the meaning depends on the project owner's profile. A tweet by a local college athlete has a smaller value than one from a high-profile professional sports player, and the awards are based on the popularity and importance of the gift. Rewards are also associated with the project itself as well. If you sponsored a project to raise funds for a local school team to compete in other countries, you could expect part of the prize to include a picture from the team at the event, perhaps by keeping posters of "thank you" on them. Many financial incentives can include naming case privileges, the name on their clothing, a listing on their website through social networks, or branded clothes.

Of course, social media plays a major part in this form of fundraising, and a reliable online presence, a good social network, and a successful website allow the project owner to build the social atmosphere required to raise the visibility of their project.

AFTER THE LAUNCH (CROWDFUNDING LAUNCH)

Beyond Raising Capital

It's not only about raising money, crowdfunding. A participant in a crowdfunding round has a mutual love for your project, a deep belief in your business to prosper, and will also support you non-financially in other ways. In a report by Nesta and the University of Cambridge, businesses that made equity crowdfunding referred to this as the highest added interest from crowdfunding investors:

1. Networking and connections: Crowdfunders will extend its business network by connecting you to network contacts. 74% of survey respondents said investors could expand their networks through introductions.

2. Marketing and Advocacy: Crowdfunding backers are also your leading brand advisors, investing in your marketing plan and staff, and helping your product achieve exposure through their network. 53% of respondents to the survey said their investors were helpful in this field.

3. Contributing expertise: If a multitude of investors supports your crowdfunding campaign, it means that you may have a large pool of mentors from different professions who can bring relevant industry knowledge and expertise to your firm, whether they are experts in expanding into a given region or knowledge of a particular function or industry.

4. Feedback and market validation: Your investors can provide valuable feedback to help you refine your product or service offerings during or after your crowdfunding campaign.

5. Support for business/product growth: 51 % of respondents said their investors even contributed their time to project or product development.

6. Effective equity crowdfunding campaigns had quite a good record of receiving follow-on financing. 71% of the equity crowdfunded companies that they sampled had secured or had talked about financing. 39% of survey respondents in the Nesta survey said their crowdfunding investors could also help in this area.

Companies who have active crowdfunding campaigns have reported similar benefits demonstrating who crowdfunding backers focused on incentives are more than just consumers that have pre-ordered the goods. If you plan to do a crowdfunding campaign, it is important that your supporters or investors make the added value available and use the full power of the crowd for your company.

Common Crowdfunding Problems and Solutions After the Launch

Entrepreneurs are often involved in starting a start-up or innovative product concept but do not have the financial resources to start up. Running a rewards-based crowdfunding campaign can be the perfect way to raise the manufacturing capital and other costs before the product or business is created. Crowdfunding primarily uses the financial assistance of others, usually in the form of orders, in exchange for free or a substantial discount upon delivery of the purchase. In return for financial backing, a more conventional lender or creditor may involve the ownership of a greater share of your company, or impose lending terms to include broad initial pay-back periods and high-interest rates.

The first step after the typical crowdfunding campaign is over is to get the product produced promptly. It is important that a manufacturer is in place and ready to begin your project and a back-up plan. If your product is viral, your manufacturer may be more demanding than they are equipped to handle, therefore have a contingency plan ready for this. Delays in delivering the product to your financial supporters can rage and ruin your company's image and can break ties to crowdfunding sites, customers, and media. One solution is to restrict the number of choices that you sell. For example, too many choices of color, size, or product type can increase manufacturing costs, especially if the minimum quantity requirements for each category are not met. In this case, profits can suffer from higher manufacturing costs, or investors may not receive their products at all, thereby damaging the reputation of your company. It is essential for a successful crowdfunding campaign to keep your product portfolio as simple and streamlined as possible.

The item crucial to the campaign 's success requires a detailed measurement of packaging and shipping costs. If shipping costs are not estimated correctly, but international shipping costs are imperative to your overall profits, and your campaign can fall by itself. Decide before launching a campaign if you want the goods to be delivered only domestically or whether you want foreign shipment.

Most Kickstarter projects have a foreign alternative and will have an exact cost estimate. Incredibly high product demand affects not only production costs but also packaging costs. This part of your campaign is best served by a shipping company. You should provide precise figures before you launch your bid and manage the entire packaging and shipping operation. As in the case of production firms, analysts who deliver completion facilities will identify those that are best able to accommodate the planned amount and those that can support you in the case of unusually strong demand.

How to Prepare for a Crowdfunding Project After the Launch

Crowdfunding is not one step, you have a pre-start, which we are discussing today, and then you are starting your campaign. After the launch of your campaign, you can live your own life, and you need to be prepared for anything that happens as your campaign evolves. The next thing is the end of your campaign and things you need to do to close it off and not least to send your supporters (if you haven't already), to thank all those who helped with your campaign and also to use the funds they raised for the project.

You might want to look at several things before you can start your Crowdfunding campaign successfully. All of them are to brace emotionally for what is to come. Get your head into the game; prepare yourself for anything your campaign could bring. You can bet that something unexpected will happen regardless of how you imagined it, so now is the time to get ready.

Then think of how the people who support your campaign will be rewarded. Will there be more and more bonuses as the gifts increase? Will you give a great gift to an ultimate giver? What is the smallest donation choice, and how is it going to be rewarded? Remember, your goal is to raise funds for your project or idea, so what kind of gifts/rewards do you want, but don't cost a lot? You could even ask your existing audience what they believe is a good reward. This allows you to early receive their support and offer an award that fits your audience.

Determine, then, how you will explain the idea to the audience clearly and convincingly. How can you say? How can you say it? Sound, video, photos? Could even you tell them all about your project and teach them how to make them benefit? Why not check to play out with family and friends? Now is the time to get the kinks together. You don't want to try to make corrections when your campaign starts.

You want to take time to practice your post or your "pitch" in the pre-launch process. You must be most enthusiastic about your idea. You are the one that can "sell" it to future backers.

Using Social Media for Raising Funds

If you collect funds for the business, it is made simpler and more successful by social media than in the past. You can reach a much wider audience now, and your results are often more efficient.

A strategy called crowdfunding is a very effective way to raise funds for the business. Crowdfunding consolidates the idea, creates a solid and attractive storyline for your idea, and encourages people who support it in a huge way. You do this through social media, viral video promotions, etc. A wonderful benefit of crowdfunding with that is it allows you to create a large user base quickly by drawing multiple micro-funders concurrently.

Now it is very easy to apply for funding via social media using fundraising widgets or badges, social networks like Twitter and Causes (which is part of Facebook). In regards to the transfers themselves, PayPal and Strong Network are both quickly and efficiently able to do so.

Without the burden of transfers and anything involved in the financing dimension, you can now focus very clearly and succinctly on delivering your message as well as on reaching the right audiences. You are concerned about communications and transactions (almost someone else) will be handled. Targeting the right people means you are looking for people that will help you spread the word on of their websites. This kind of union is very effective and will not eat much of your budget.

Tools available

There are nowadays many resources to help you collect funds for your business. Some of the devices are intended to work better for SMEs, and other instruments are designed to work for small to big organizations more efficiently.

The following are some of the most effective instruments for financing small businesses in particular:

Kickstarter: The philosophy of Kickstarter is that a good idea that is properly communicated has the potential to spread widely and quickly. The tool is based on the premise that a significant number of people can provide funding and support. Kickstarter does not launch a project unless it is fully funded. This reduces the risk of loss. This is a tool that motivates people to engage in different projects for all kinds of reasons.

GlobalGiving: an online philanthropy marketplace where people can post an idea and finance it. GlobalGiving links donors in the U.S. and abroad to community-based projects that need support. As a donor, you select the project you wish to support, contribute (tax withholding) and receive progress reports on a regular basis so that you can see what your money pays for exactly.

ChipIn: This is amongst the most popular widgets for distributed fundraising by fundraisers now. The app can be built on your website and social media profile pages, really user-friendly. Basically, it is a "donate" button with a thermometer that tests the campaign success. You can log in to ChipIn for free, but you must set up a PayPal account to accept donations.

Changing the Present: It is a non-profit agency that connects you to 1500 valuable and unusual presents such as "adopt a tiger for $40" and "stop global warming for $20." ChangingThePresent encourages donors through their homepage to make donations for all amounts. The most valuable rate is 100 million monthlies.

Causes: This is handled by Facebook and is a perfect way to attract attention to important purposes. This allows fundraisers to ask for donations from their contacts and recruit volunteers who also want to participate in a particular cause. For social reasons, many people can use the website and engage in fundraising ideas by posting Causes profiles on their own Facebook page.

SixDegrees: This is a Network for Good partner that facilitates careful social networking. You could support your favorite causes by creating or donating fundraising badges on the site. You should also find out the reasons for certain individuals. The methods used by SixDegrees make it simple to have. The progress of your case can be checked at the top of the badge.

Razoo: It's a unique way to raise money online. If you want to run a fundraiser for someone else's sake, raise funds for your own company or donate money, Rozoo will provide you with basic resources to help you accomplish your goals. It allows supporters to discover useful and motivating opportunities and supports organizations in various ways.

PincGiving: This helps charities and businesses to achieve their philanthropic objectives. In the United States, the United Kingdom, and Australia, you will send the charity of your choosing. You can also raise funds through your own homepage and create a fundraising campaign for peer-to-peer funding or access millions of dollars of grants (in your preferred currency).

SocialVibe: This is a social media micro-funding program that links non-profit organizations, companies, and users. This enables them to engage with different sponsors and share branded content. You do not have to donate any money if you use the service because corporate sponsors make all the donations. You will be encouraged, however, to spend advertising space on your social networks by adding the social media profile pages with SocialVibe widget.

There are also numerous effective instruments for greater fundraising efforts:

Artez: It offers a collection of online fundraising resources to tailor your fundraising plan to the company's unique needs. People can just make donations and buy tickets for a particular event.

Care2: It is an online group whose participants regularly participate in environmental and social concerns and provide a fundraising and advocacy forum. The alliance between non-profit groups, philanthropists, and socially conscious corporations to benefit others is a very successful means of collecting money and funding very important causes.

Convio: This tool provides non-profit organizations with fundraising, marketing, advocacy, and a database with donor tools. Convio's module allows users to take their view and translate it into online or integrated marketing programs that collect, engage, and transform people into loyal contributors. Person and team fundraiser accounts can be built, and reporting and analytical capabilities are available.

A fundraising campaign has several elements to make it a success. Some of these components include a call for action that specifically calls for contributions and sends a message to those who might want to become involved. This is an easy way to donate money (by credit card, it is immediately linked with the advertisements and collected to the organization's website requesting the funds.

Many of the organizations which were referred to here are excellent and also can help you make a real difference. They are easy to use and navigate, and you should give them an attempt to see which works the best for you and the business.

CAMPAIGN CONCLUSION (CROWDFUNDING CAMPAIGN)

Effective Ways of Non-Profit Fund-Raising Year Around

Efficient forms to raise funds without profit

Most NGOs fail to collect money each year. Even with several donors, non-profit organizations do their job successfully every year. Most groups go to sleep all year long because of the lack of funding and volunteers. Good utilization of money improves the efficiency of an organization to accomplish positive goals and to benefit people. The following are among the proposals to raise funds successfully throughout the year and retain consistent funding for donors.

Create a straightforward mission statement: Let us know what the company wants to do and whether the public will take part in the mission. The audience is excited to be part of the organization with positive goals and strong vision, and the society will support the mission. Vaguely defined services and intermittent assistance would be minimal. The clarity in the statement of mission increases awareness among people from all walks of life. Focus on a mission statement that is readily understood before the big fundraising efforts. Don't forget to protect the values that you support during the year.

Recruit active members of the board: The majority of non-profit agencies in the recruiting board members market struggle miserably. In the majority of cases, family or friends serve as board members with limited knowledge, time, and resources. Also, if they are grateful for their involvement, professional leadership is important to assign individuals to work reasonably effectively to accomplish goals in a fair amount of time. Knowing and resourceful individuals, who will consistently contribute to a project and collaborate with one another as a team, drive an organization to greater heights and help accomplish its goals. Many individuals are committed to non-profit activities; seek to hire these people into the company. Dissolve current board members if necessary to create more truly functional board members. The organization's founder often becomes more of a threat than a treasure. In such situations, please reduce the role of the founder and seek assistance from the consultants.

Personalize the challenge of achieving a competitive edge: With the many businesses vying for corporate interest and awarding capital, the company has to have a competitive advantage. Inform people that you are behind a cause and that you are searching for assistance to carry out your goal. A unique background behind a campaign makes supporters more appealing than joining an anonymous project. Do not go crazy on this mission, as many promoters and board members neglect the fundamental existence of an organization.

Have a strategic plan: aid experts develop action strategies. Provide a strategic plan. Create strategic plans in advance for optimal management of available resources. Be diligent in organizing activities with minimal budgets for your company. Extravagant services are not expected to collect funds successfully year-round. Strategic strategies associated with a strategic strategy for the organization provide the company with long-term assistance. Fundraising activities distributed over the entire year to different projects are more successful than intermittent initiatives.

Create information about the organization: Detecting individuals through different media is the secret to any successful fundraising effort. Speak about the group, its goals, strategies, and purpose in the local community through social media, the Internet, radio, TV, and newspapers to supporters and the public at large. The best ways to increase awareness are local libraries, community centers, and colleges (depending on the cause and whether colleges permit). Do not hesitate to speak on behalf of the organization, its missions. It is a smart idea to launch an advertising drive well in advance of the fundraiser event so that the contributions are enhanced.

Precise financial objectives: Most donors complain about the mismanagement of their contributions and struggle to access the vulnerable efficiently. To prevent these questions, state specifically the financial situation and have competent assistance in handling the funds. Periodically send financial statements to donors to ensure transparency. Understand your financial prospects when engaging in big events. The detailed outline of a business strategy and the necessary financial capital allows other donors to support and maintain organizations. If the company does not meet any budgetary goals for the year, the Executive Board may try to look at plans for potential ventures.

Effective use of media: radio, print, Internet, and television can be used. If you're still on a really low budget, first select free things. Substantial activities, such as door-to-door awareness and baking activities, will help spread the word locally. Use the Internet effectively to disseminate information, be aware of privacy concerns before sending emails, newsletters, or fundraising requests. Save capital as part of joint campaigns with other companies. Search your local newspaper, radio, and television websites for free advertising sections. Many churches help local non-profits to advertise freely and use these advantages before putting money into social media advertising.

Make your website searchable easily by optimizing the search engine (SEO). Set up a PayPal citizen donation page. Do not impose fixed amounts on your website for donors; it irritates and restricts most donors if some are willing to donate. This is not a very smart idea to place a price tag on your project when you look for monetary support. You improve your brand by using your website as a major marketing and information tool.

If you have a Facebook or Google+ page, start publishing your cause and get the community involved before you start fund applications. You shouldn't be restricted to Facebook, LinkedIn, Pinterest, or Twitter ads by the media. There are several forums, associations, and groups that sponsor and support non-profit organizations individually and acknowledge these connections to boost your efforts. Start fundraising at the grassroots level to gain civic support and people's engagement to improve the brand. Sometimes flying camps, garage sales, lemonade stands, and cookie drives can help raise more money than Facebook or Twitter advertising.

Prepare Brand Ambassadors: individuals are really quickly sharing the positive news. Educate friends and Share the passion, family, and community to become ambassadors for your brand to raise funds. Start an ambitious campaign to create and promote your cause. If your friends and family support your missions, it is also a clear message to the public to place their confidence in your mission. Past volunteers are your organization's most valuable asset; keep them regularly informed about your missions. Hold volunteer lunches/dinners to show how committed you are to the company and support them. Encourage people to join in the activities with their community and families.

Crowdfunding: This is one of the most common and modern fundraising strategies used by many NGOs. Crowdfunding is a compilation or a pool of small funds raised by average citizens to finance a project or campaign or a specific cause. There are several dedicated crowdfunding sites to help people collect money all year round. Huteera.com allows non-profits, for example, only to raise funds by registering the cause! Get your trigger information. Sites such as razoo.com enable you to create fundraising events for any reason, whether personal or non-profit. Effective YouTube videos and other web pages are also enticing choices!

Effective communication and planning will certainly attract financial assistance throughout the year. The most successful way to maintain consistent cash flow is to obtain skilled planners' support in collecting short- and long-term funds. Nonetheless, if there are continuous funding and good planning, any non-profit agency will reap capital. Successful board members, along with volunteers, are the key source of raising funds!

Crowdfunding for a Business Is More Than Just Money

Start-ups and small business owners often see massive increases in crowdfunding in recent years. Today, it is one of the most popular ways business owners can fund their business without going to a bank to request a conventional loan. Naturally, crowdfunding doesn't really stop anyone coming to a bank for a business loan.

It makes sense for everyone, though, to carefully prepare their strategy and meet all their financial requirements using a successful crowdfunding campaign mostly on the right platform. For those who believe crowdfunding is only one way to raise funds from various people, they have to think about it again.

Crowdfunding is more than just raising money.

A lot easier than traditional financing

Traditional financing for entrepreneurs, as well as small business owners, is quite a challenge. You get to know rich people, banks, venture capitalists, angel investors, and other lending agencies as soon as you are at a point where it is needed to collect funds for your business. The problem here is that you start on the width of the funnel and narrow down to find the right investors on the point side of the funnel. If you cannot make a deal with your final option, you'll lose all your time and effort.

Crowdfunding, on the other hand, is the exact opposite of conventional funding. You start at the end of the funnel, start your crowdfunding campaign and let the right people find you. Those who find the concept attractive as well as attractive are going to invest. You won't have to go door to door to find the right person to make investments in your company and your idea. This facilitates crowdfunding much more than traditional financing.

Great business forecast

In order to maximize the odds of having the right investor on the side, you need to see the prospective investors at every location, conference, and meeting. But you can only go so far in the limited time before somebody else copies and capitalizes on your idea. On the other hand, you do not have to focus on your activities and promotion to help fuel your company financially. The first step of crowdsourcing is to find the right platform, as many are available.

The crowdfunding site has to be selected based on its success and public usability. In short, you benefit from the platform's business growth. If the crowdfunding site is popular on several continents, you could expect your money to come from all over the world.

Less risk than conventional funds

One of the biggest problems with traditional financing, especially risk capital, is that this funding involves a lot of risks. Venture capitalists are individuals or institutions often more interested in their very own financial gain than in watching the business grow. Their purpose is and double or triple to there investment in your company. Therefore, they also have very stringent investment-related regulations. If you have any concerns about the idea 's progress, they will always want to send you money as a repayable loan-the rule are always tight.

If you think your product/service would prosper tremendously, you will try to enter into perpetual royalty arrangements or attempt to get away as much equity as possible in the company.

Those who finance your company through crowdfunding may not even ask for any participation in your company. Their donations may be as low as 5 dollars, and they do not expect much in exchange. Often they would spend heavily without having much equity. Their incentives are always as easy as a free product preview.

Professionalism brings you out.

Just because crowdfunding is less risky than conventional financing doesn't mean you can all be casual. To ask the world to invest in your idea is a big company, so to persuade people to invest in, you must be at your best. The first thing you have to do is build a clear business strategy. Secondly, you want a team of right professionals with whom you can look and trust. If your team's air is negative, you won't be invested with a single dollar. You must also have a better explanation of where you are going to spend your money.

Bring them to the front if you have samples. Build videos to show the inventions. Be sure that a solution to a current issue is your product/service. Do not create a problem, and then fix it. Angel investors frequently use crowdfunding platforms and must ensure that they invest in people and companies that are serious and not a hobby.

Support you build a follower group.

There is a great deal of investment in crowdfunding websites as small contributions. These people really aren't investors, and they are ordinary people who like an idea and want to see it practically. You think your idea can solve one of their problems or perhaps make the world a better place. If you can persuade them that either or all of those things are your ideas, they would then actively invest in them. Such individuals are early adopters for your technology/product/service and are also word of mouth promoters for your brand.

Final Thoughts

It is not a coincidence which crowdfunding is now one of the most popular ways to support growth, marketing, and growth through crowdfunding for new businesses and entrepreneurs. They must see some advantages of financing their efforts by crowding conventional funds. If you are someone who is taking the same path, the first advice would be to select a platform with confidence, reputation, and outreach for the crowdfunding campaign.

Finance Your Startup in the Community

Financing your project will be safer through your own culture. Your "community" may be related, geographical, interest-related, or affiliated.

The Funded Business Sector is not an agreed word. However, there are more and more ways businesses are supported financially within a community. Some of them are very traditional, such as coops that began in the 19th century, and new ones are constantly emerging. One example is crowd financing, which comes from the social networking phenomenon very recently.

The momentum comes from two directions. The first is Wall Street's disaffection, and all that is "big banking." The other is the rising 'local' trend, the true heirs of ecological.

Maintaining funding in your own community has benefits and disadvantages. Some of the advantages are that you know people provide money and your company is 'visible' to them. Banks are very bureaucratic, and lending decisions have to be 'passed' somewhere else to a corporate office. Your access to the borrowers is simple with mutual support and would be face to face in most situations. The reverse of that coin includes minuses: you'll have no place to 'hide.' I still say 'over-communicate' lenders with their banks. If you borrow from those you love, you typically spend a lot of your time (and emotion) in dealing with them.

Family and friends (some say, fools, too)

For many generations, startups have looked for finance, be it equity or loan money, from their family and friends. Often this also applies to customers and suppliers. The Angel Capital Investment Foundation reports that startups receive 60 billion dollars annually from peers and family. This is probably the largest single source of 'series A' funding.

There are strong reservations about this journey because emotion and relationships are in the foreground. You should concentrate on getting the capital, but you will need to know your views. Treat them as if they were a corporation and giving them a reason to benefit. Be sure that you pay them back and use a promissory statement to make them legal.

Get a contingency plan. Contingency account. If you have to call the loan from a family member for reasons such as the lender has lost a job, you must be able to repay quickly or risk family feud. Ask yourself if this is first of all the right course and beware that it's difficult to price the right deal for both parties and structure it. Consider how things are going to be if your startup goes down. Downside risk management is also the secret to a good project.

Financed Community Business

Agriculture supported by the Community (CSA) now provides small-scale financial support to farmers. In general, members of the community purchase shares on farms before the season and receive deliveries on and when the specific crops or meat is available. The process has now spread to other economic sectors, especially in the agro-food sector. Seafood (Port Clyde, ME) and restaurants where consumers pay and get reimbursed over time for meals and other rewards are some examples.

This appears to be a rather effective but somewhat costly way to collect funds for the investor. I was losing several hundred dollars to support a small bookstore in my village where my first money was repaid monthly on a small amount of interest in books. The business model was not carefully prepared, and the startup was poorly managed and failed.

Interestingly, two years later, another community-supported business opened in the space next door-a restaurant. They not only sold shares to local supporters but also purchased products from local CSA farms. In addition to the CSA model of pre-financing product sales by subscription or 'shares,' there are many other ways.

Collaboratives

They are much more popular than you might expect, locally as well as nationally. Nearly 30,000 of them are in the United States. I used to be a two-store retailer on the board of the Brattleboro Food Coop in my local city of Vermont. With 16 million dollars in turnover, we had reached capacity in our main store and decided to build a new store at the cost of several million dollars. Coops in the area provided loans for 3 and 5 years for well over $1 million as part of the shareholder equity to support the bank and another financing. In addition, another local coop – Coop Power – partnered in the building by supplying the solar roof.

A significant majority of coops are small and geographically focused. Most of them belong to farmers and banks. In effect, the Savings and Loan Associations are co-ops. Some have started small and local but have become big corporations with local funding. One example is Land lakes, now almost a national dairy brand.

Public Direct Offers

For a company to "go public" without an intermediary who orchestrates an IPO, a direct public offering is away. A corporation completes paperwork and disclosures needed to enable it to sell shares directly to the market-shareholders and the society of the firm.

Quimper Mercantile, in Port Townsend, WA, has earned more than $500,000 in a DPO to open a general store, is a recent example of DPO.

Cutting Edge Capital helped them. A more client of CEC is the People's Community Market, whose entrepreneurial entrepreneurship program enables Californians of all economic backgrounds to create a grocery market in West Oakland and become owners and shareholders.

Funding of the crowd

This year's Employment Act requires any person to spend up to $ 10,000 a year or up to 10 percent of his or her net profit in private firms, whether he or she makes less than $100,000 a year. This compares with the current as crowdfunders are pretty much non-financially compensated. EarlyShares, an equity-based crowdfunding platform, is one of the first platforms off the block.

Income-based financing and customer financing

Another new way to finance is revenue-based finance. The assumption is that the investor takes a loss on its profits, rather than the loss associated with the development in investment, by paying a percentage of the top line. A US company called RevenueLoan now offers a revenue-based financing product for startups but on relatively large sums. Revenue Based Financing (RBF) is a hybrid financing method that satisfies the need for businesses with about $1 million to $10 million of income and a proven growth plan in the growth capital market.

Group Builder

The makers' subculture 's common focus involves engineering-oriented methods such as computing, robotics, 3D printing, 2D plotter cuts, water jet cuts, and the use of CNC machines (even in brodering) as well as more conventional acts such as metalwork, woodworking, and mainstream arts and craft.

The entire print-on-demand industry is another example in which authors are able to produce books on an individual basis. While they are not funding agencies, they reduce the costs associated with small scale manufacturing; however, hybrids combine factory facilities with startup seed funding and factory-like incubation space.

Incubators and Business Accelerators

Enterprises wishing to enter a business incubation program must register for membership. They tend to be actual locations where you can launch a business under a single roof. Many incubators/accelerators are affordable for entry, and even only seed funding has been distributed.

Business accelerators can focus on very specific geographies (such as cities or states), industries (such as information technology or clean power), industrial processes (such as manufactured kitchens or industrial kitchens), and accelerators can offer physical space on short-term or media settings.

Many incentives for Mutual financing

There are much other community or 'local' financing opportunities. Financial incentives may exist, such as grants from local government agencies or competitions for business plans conducted by local development bodies or academic institutions.

Depending on your startup's governance structure, program funds may be accessible. For example, in the countries where the L3C (limited responsibility company that limits profit level) form exists, you can receive basic funding.

There are also combinations of various ways of funding the community. You could use crowdfunding, for example, to extend the route for family and friends. You can add other people to the network, and each contributor's risk can be reduced by a larger lender base because they will supply smaller sums. The downside of the hybrid is the time you need to make lenders aware of progress.

How do you do it?

Brainstorm with friends and partners, but do that in an organized manner. You have probably fixed ideas about how to raise capital for your company, so it is necessary to create new ideas. One of the tools I use is mind mapping (a variety of free software and programs available on the

Web). It helps me to quickly capture in one visual space all of my dispersed thoughts. It helps me to see the trees in the wood.

Affinity diagrams may be anything in a category that you can use. It sounds frightening, but everything you need is some wall space and adhesive notes. Participants work on and post their own ideas. If you have them all on the wall, you can start to see which ideas are connected or which can create new ideas.

Be as crazy as you can on where money or credit will come from. You would be surprised how many sources there are and how many people are interested in helping.

Equity Crowdfunding: Set to Change the World

I am surprised at how little understanding exists regarding crowdfunding and the huge differences between the donation crowdfunding that has existed for several years and equity crowdfunding in the very short term. We keep very close tabs of what's happening in the world of crowdfunds, and while I read the various chapter in major publications or view segment TV news.

Let me then take a moment to attempt to clarify. Donation crowdfunding is very easy. People effectively "donate" money to a company or cause without ownership expectations. In return, they earn a monetary "award," and the prizes are usually granted in amounts depending on how much they give. A modest pledge could lead to a reward with a bumper sticker or a T-Shirt, while a significant donation might include goods for the first edition, a weekend trip paying for all costs, or an invitation for an exclusive celebrity launch party. These sites, such as Kickstarter and hundreds more, receive a percentage fee from earned funds-typically 5-10 percent.

But equity crowdfunding is a completely different and, frankly, much more exciting animal. Equity investing has the power to turn the world of financing directly into one another, supplying regular buyers and small private entrepreneurs with easy entry-excluding financial intermediaries who have for decades been cornering the private investment sector and lining up their pockets.

The biggest difference between stock and donation crowdfunding is that the donors are fully owned by the company in return for their donations-whether it is stock shares or LLC units. So rather than t-shirts from the latest round of industry leaders like Google, LinkedIn, Facebook, or Twitter, customers will take part in the next round of emerging market growth (and yes, failure).

There are some important safeguards to raise capital through equity crowdfunding, however: most companies will have to draw up their business plan, a financial model or audited/certified financial statements, an assessment of their equity offering, and several other items to list their offer on an SEC-approved website platform.

This new access to capital is likely to significantly support the next wave of new businesses. Rather than a small pool of investors to invest in new businesses, billions of people around the world will soon be able to fund tomorrow's start-ups.

As things stand, there are already significant changes in US securities laws in the area of equity crowdfunding for the first time, and companies can collect capital from accredited investors (people with substantial annual salaries or gross value) via equity crowdfunding. And equity crowd funders can advertise their agreements to accredited investors, a so-called "general demand." This has not been permitted in the United States since the 1920s.

The third and last piece of the stock crowdfunding puzzle is when the SEC lays down the rules allowing non-accredited investors to fund equity crowdfunding. That would be the primary priority for us to be permitted to invest in private companies. It's a Great DEAL if the rules for collecting this kind of capital are not too complicated.

Now the most interesting thing about this case is to continue and foresee and grasp what will happen after this third and final piece of the equity crowdfunding puzzle has come into being, which will take place sometime in the 2nd quarter of 2014.

First of all, behind the scenes, a lot of technology has been designed to brace for the activities that are basically under consideration. Institutional investors are not stupid-others have been pouring capital into the platforms and other companies that would help equity crowdfunding. Others also sought to build a secondary market for crowdfunding investment to resell, which will give the equity crowdfunding business and exposure to buyers – making the investment much more appealing.

And not only institutional investors take bold steps. Social media companies, media/publishers and others have also jacketed by acquiring or building capacity on the company's stock crowdfunding infrastructure.

If you reflect on the rise of the personal computer market in the 1980s and the emergence of the Internet in the mid-1990s, then the maritime shift in the financial sector is as, if not more, prolific. The world changed forever when Netscape created and launched the first web browser in 1995. The number of web users grew from 16 million in early 1996 to 360 million at the end of 2000. The share prices of recently formed firms like Amazon, eBay, Yahoo, and Priceline have risen by as much as 100 times between 1996 and 2000. The same is likely to happen to businesses that represent the large capital crowdfunding market.

DELIVER THE REWARDS – (CROWDFUNDING FULFILLMENT)

What's the Next Step If Your Crowdfunding Campaign Fails?

Have you got a GREAT idea as well as a cause? If you think you have an incredible idea ... Great! Great. Now, we need to uncover the root cause of why you haven't achieved your fundraising objective. There could be a number of factors, and many of them we are going to talk about. But if you think about the campaign and you're not sure that the idea was great, then STOP right there. Don't continue that campaign. Don't continue. Go another way, or wait until some other brilliant idea comes into your head!

With the right platform, were you? All websites with crowdfunding are NOT the same. You have to compare the prices of each website. Can you keep all of your donations on your platform or just the amount if you achieve your goal? Does your website have a short timeline for raising money? Can you change the campaign target amounts? Will your company have exemplary customer service and support? During your first campaign, you might not have thought of all these questions, but now you know how to ask yourself. Make a chart. Make a chart. List your options for the crowdfunding site ... And go from there. And go from there. Which platform offers the best value-added services for you with all the other services.

Did you prepare yourself before you come alive? Did you just wake up one morning and ask, "Oh, I guess I'm going to collect new pink boots money?" Well, that won't work. There is a lot of effort and resources to excel in a fundraiser program. You consider only to write your plan, do the pre-work. Talk to all your friends and family. Tell them that you need these pink socks, where you buy them, what's so cool about these socks, where to get them and who really gets them. Starting a "Help me Raise Pink Boots Money" campaign is one thing ... Starting with a campaign, "My name is Moses, and I'm raising $500 to buy the most incredibly soft rose boots for five children in the children's hospital here in Reno to recover from cancer. Because the flow of their blood is slower and the temperatures in their bodies lower, they'll keep their toes tasty and their spirits high. If you have sent these two different emails ... What answer do you think you were going to get? More details can be given to your crowd AFTER you start the campaign, the MORE effective YOUR campaign is! Begin planning research before you launch another program.

Have you got a crowd? We were over it before, but you need a crowd, really. You have no 5200 friends on Facebook, but you do have to think of a crowd to help fund your campaign. It's not enough to continue the initiative. It's NOT enough to post it on Facebook once a week and tweet it out. You must make people WOULD care what you care about. Encourage them to support drive your peak. Cultivate the network for your campaign to launch.

Have you got a plan? Are you like Julie Roberts in Pretty Lady, a kind of girl (or guy) "Fly by the seat of my pants" OR, do you have a schedule for your latest campaign? If you are organized and evaluated by definition isn't important, but you DO have to be organized and prepare for a crowdfunding campaign to achieve the highest results. You must PLAN what your crowdfunding strategy is going to be. How many times are you going to update your campaign? How much are you going to share it on social networks? Are you going to send out a press release? Do you like to contact your local news agencies? So much are your personal and technical connections going via email? Will you give your campaign any rewards? When are you going to thank your supporters? Have you changed everything in your plan since you got input from friends and family?

Was your purpose realistic and relevant? Did you set your fundraising objective to achieve what you would like or NEEDED to complete the project? Your supporters will know if you ask for too much money, and they're going to wonder what you do with any excess. Place your targets in phases if necessary. This helps you to achieve little success on the way ... Enhance YOUR principle and excite your fans to help you hit the landmark. It's no risk to press $500 for those black socks ... And when you achieve that, update to thank everyone and tell them you're going to raise your goal to 700 $now and buy two more pairs of that currency.

Please take care of these things. Take a notebook and write scratch ideas and create a new attack plan. You, Will, continue anew if you think you have a Brilliant idea or an Inspirational initiative. Take advantage of past experience to know what to do and not what to do this time!

Three Powerful Tricks to Slingshot Your Crowdfunding Campaign

In this chapter, we will address the three things you have to do to help fire the success of your crowdfunding campaign. Before you start your crowdfunding campaign, you should understand that these are things to do.

The first thing you need to do is build a blog, there are a lot of resources, but the one I suggest is a WordPress blog. This is available for free by visiting wordpress.org or registering a domain of your own, preferably one that relates to what is going to be your project and setting up a WordPress blog on your own domain.

Instead, you want to set up a Twitter account and use this page to start messaging your future supporters. Your Twitter account, in combination with your WordPress blog, would have been the basis for communicating with potential supporters.

Then you want to reach backers, people who might benefit from the project. Once you've developed your blog, you want to continue with a couple of posts about your project. Additionally, once you've posted each of these blog posts, you may want to comment on your Twitter page so you can get an idea of how it works. You are set up and ready to go after you've done this.

What you want to do now is to email anyone you think is a possible sponsor of your idea. Now that's not to contact anyone in the world, it means to contact people or anyone you think will be interested in, so places to contact will be forums, other blogs and follow other people on Twitter.

For example, say you created a new gardening tool, so you want to go to gardening forums, online people, Twitter bloggers, and gardeners. You'll get in contact with them, tell them what you're doing, chat about your idea and schedule and get them to follow you on Twitter. You'll also get them to read your blog and something like that.

So, what you're going to do with is you build up a follow-up slowly. There may not be much of a following, but these people are committed and really interested in what you do. What you are doing here is to create a base to launch your crowdfunding ventures. You should be able to touch the ground by doing these three things when it is time to launch your crowdfunding program.

Is Crowdfunding Right for Your Non-Profit?

Non-profits do not rely solely on conventional ways of fundraising today. Technology has made use of some genuinely whimsical fundraising options. One of them was crowdfunding. The strategy is based on the concept of gathering small funds from several individuals over the Internet.

In addition to the money you have earned, you collect a handful of donors supporting your cause or initiative. But is this a safe and effective way to rely on it? Should non-profits focus on this fundraising concept?

You have to learn about crowdfunding and how the fundraising takes place to address these questions. You need to ensure that the cause you collect funds has a fixed duration. It is not a reasonable choice for the raising of long-term funds. The methodology is ideally suited for projects that need financing at a defined time.

When you decide to get your cause crowdfunded, you have to organize a non-profit crowdfunding campaign. The initiative will be tailored and provide all the pertinent material about the non-profit and cause.

You will be able to cover the upfront expenses to collect funds. Crowdfunding, as such, requires no capital expenses, but it definitely takes your time and effort to make your campaign successful. You will need a team that can build a stunning tale, post your social media strategy, quantifies input, and track if appropriate. You will always deeply focus on the benefits you would give your supporters. To reduce the cost, you should consider providing your backers with intangible rewards, which otherwise cannot afford and reward your backers.

Getting crowdfunded will help you with additional donors and existing non-profit contributors. You need to leverage the influence of your current supporters by enabling them to increase the momentum of your campaign. Crowdfunding is often seen by organizations as a way of raising small or large individual donations, rather than as a way of catching donors outside the reach like youth and the extended circle of the existing donors.

You will have an enticing story to captivate the audience. People contribute only to campaigns with which they feel connected. A narrative plays a significant part in controlling people's hearts to commit to the initiative. When the supporter contributes to your campaign, he will necessarily share it with others.

Social media plays a significant part in crowdfunding. Your non-profit team must be sufficiently effective in managing social media. It gives you better opportunities to engage and opportunities for your company to grow.

Things to Consider When Crowdfunding for Charity

In the past, an investor had to get a lift from a business. If the idea was for a weird innovation or a modern mobile device, it always took corporate funding to get them up and to run. Such days are long past due to crowdfunding in large part.

Briefly speaking,

In short, crowdfunding, also known as crowdsourcing, is an initiative or campaign to provide financial support for a given project. The campaign is aimed at the general public to identify people or groups willing to help start the project from the drawing area to reality. These donors, in turn, receive donations or first dibs on new products after the completion of the project.

No boundaries

Crowdsourcing is not limited to technologies or applications today. Many non-profit and humanitarian organizations, or simply individuals who campaign for a single cause, have used the Internet and its billions of users as a convenient solution to the quest for desperately needed funding and money.

Objectives

The benefit of crowdsourcing is that it is targeted at individuals who care passionately for a particular cause and who otherwise would not be able to hear about the campaign if it was not for the Internet. It primarily includes social media and philanthropy.

ABC crowdfunding

Creating a fundraising initiative by crowdfunding is no rocket science. However, certain considerations must be considered in order to ensure its success.

First of all, a legitimate reason should be at the core of any initiative. It impressively means one that tugs the emotions of the demographic target.

Original

For nets that are used to hoaxing and false news, a campaign that runs on a superficial or hollow premise is quite easy to spot. This makes it important to build a true and credible crowdsourcing website. The fact is that the drive to give money can only be made possible if a connection between the advocate or cause and the donor seems to be established. Otherwise, the message of the advertisement would undoubtedly fall on deaf ears.

Technical issues

Certain technical concerns also need to be taken seriously. For example, the success of a crowdfunding campaign depends heavily on the number of visitors. As such, it is important to email and shares the word on social networks. It is critical that as many people as possible hear the campaign. The larger the target, the more likely it is to collect pledges and donations.

Money Channel

It is also a significant consideration of how the money is passed from the lender to the fund and eventually to the beneficiary or beneficiaries. How are credit card donations going to be made? What bank will obtain the funds? How long are controls to be cleared? Clear rules on these issues will be in place.

And ultimately, it is just as important to thank crowd contributors who have taken the time to fund them. Whether it's a personalized thank you card or a donation, it's a great way to send love to donors to seal a wonderful partnership.

CONCLUSION

Crowdfunding campaigns use online platforms. These platforms allow you to run your campaign from the center and take a small percentage back.

These platforms are also where you send your community or "crowd" when your project is financed. A big part of getting the money you are looking for is to make things personal for your campaign. People want to help others, not just ideas. If you like the person who runs the idea or project, you really can get behind it.

Make sure that you are all in your crowd, that you will do everything you need to obtain money, and then get your project off the ground. Nobody wants to support someone who's just halfway. You can't get a foot in and a foot out, you must get a booth.

Tell your fans how you got the idea, where did everything come from? Then tell them how and where you 're going to get there. Be transparent, be honest, and truthful. You want to be somebody you can trust to give money to. Let them see what inspired you first of all to make a Crowdfund.

Let's face it, and there's always a crowdfunding drive. Backers would like to know who is behind the project; what kind of outcomes are they going to achieve in what timeframe; what are the plans when you raise more money than going, and why should they be involved in the fight against someone else. Crowdfunding is an exchange of money, so the more you feel that you can trust, the more likely you are.

This funding will go way farther than dollars. People who embark on your campaign can spread the word and make others support your efforts. A few key supporters in social media communication can boost your Crowdfunding campaign to the "funded" category.

www.ingramcontent.com/pod-product-compliance
Lightning Source LLC
Chambersburg PA
CBHW050010230526
45465CB00003BB/1344